Finding Hope in Hopelessness

Finding Hope in Hopelessness

A Faith-Based and Clinical Conversation on Overcoming Adversity

Anthony P. Acampora
and Eric Oakes

RESOURCE *Publications* • Eugene, Oregon

FINDING HOPE IN HOPELESSNESS
A Faith-Based and Clinical Conversation on Overcoming Adversity

Resource Publications
An Imprint of Wipf and Stock Publishers
199 W. 8th Ave., Suite 3
Eugene, OR 97401

www.wipfandstock.com

PAPERBACK ISBN: 978-1-6667-3895-7
HARDCOVER ISBN: 978-1-6667-3896-4
EBOOK ISBN: 978-1-6667-3897-1

05/05/22

We are dedicating this book to the families and loved ones of those who have been lost as a result of substance use and mental health disorders. These issues do not discriminate and have impacted incalculable lives not only in the United States but also throughout the world. If we can put the differences aside, and, instead, focus on delivering real hope, those who are suffering will be the beneficiaries of our collaborative efforts for the greater good.

Contents

Acknowledgements

Eric

I would like to first and foremost thank Anthony Acampora for his dedication to this project and for inviting me to participate. His faith is an inspiration. I would like to thank my family for their constant love and support. They are my purpose. Lastly, I would like to thank the leadership and all of my colleagues at Banyan Treatment Centers for years of service helping people.

Anthony

Most importantly I wish to acknowledge my true LORD and Savior Jesus Christ. This book, nor would anything else, have been possible without God intervening in my life. I would like to acknowledge Banyan Chief Executive Officer, Joe Tuttle, and Sr. Executive Vice President and Chief Operations Officer, Eric Oakes. Joe and Eric took a leap of faith back in 2015 to start our Faith in Recovery program which has recently been expanded nationwide to all Banyan Centers at all levels of care. Joe Tuttle and Eric Oakes have been amazing leaders, mentors, and friends to me throughout the years. I am honored to be a part of this incredible organization. I also wish to thank the amazing team of professionals at Wipf and Stock Publishers with whom I have had the pleasure to work on three book publications. Tremendous thanks to Lauren Connolly for always being a source of encouragement throughout my years at Banyan. In addition, many thanks to Laura Lyons for all of her technical support. Finally, I want to acknowledge and thank our tireless editor and friend, Krissie Schuster Cilano.

Abbreviations

AACC	American Association Christian Counselors
ABC	American Broadcasting Network
ABS	American Bible Society
AMBER	America's Missing: Broadcast Emergency Response
BBC	British Broadcasting Corporation
CDC	Centers for Disease Control
CEO	Chief Executive Officer
COO	Chief Operating Officer
COVID	Coronavirus disease
ESV	English Standard Version
MADD	Mothers Against Drunk Driving
NASB	New American Standard Bible
NIV	New International Version
NKJV	New King James Version
NLT	New Living Translation
PTSD	Post Traumatic Stress Disorder

Introduction

*"Come to me, all you who are weary and
burdened, and I will give you rest."*
—*MATTHEW 11:28 NIV*

*"What one must not do is to rule out the
supernatural as the one impossible explanation."*
—*CS LEWIS*

THE POINT OF THIS book is to relate a conversation between two
people who see things differently but are willing to talk about
those differences. We want to create a safe place to talk about religion and social science, and to actually enter the space where they
converge. We do this in the name of helping all people, not just
the ones who agree with us. We want people to have their own
conversations about wellness and healing. We want this conversation to be helpful, easy, and brief. We wanted to address topics
that people may find a little interesting, making no prediction as to
its profundity. It is the final desire that someone, somewhere, sees
hope where they hadn't before.

Introduction

Please understand that if you want help with feeling better, thinking differently about things, or looking at things in a different way, you need not wait until you are forced to do it. Neither is it too late, if you find yourself with a crisis, to get started anywhere you can. We encourage you to start by talking to someone. Have a conversation with a person you trust or take a leap and talk to a professional.

It's a tough time to talk about anything. Sometimes it feels like every day is an exercise in walking on eggshells. As children, we were taught never to discuss religion or politics. Now it seems like there is nothing that isn't about religion or politics. There is so much division in this, our time of living. We hear everywhere that the rift between those on one side and those on the other side is irreparable. Anthony and I have spoken at length about this, as friends and colleagues, and have discovered something. We think it's as much about how we approach our conversations as it is our beliefs behind them. When you think about it, it is virtually impossible for there to be only two sides to an issue, yet we tend to approach our relationships as if there are only two ways to look at everything—our way or the wrong way.

Here is our attempt to look at things a little differently. Read this book as a conversation between two people. Anthony is an ordained minister, and a chaplain and faith director in our national drug treatment centers. I am a therapist, a social worker, and an administrator in those same treatment centers. In our conversations, we are asking each other to give our version of the truth on the subjects of hope and its obstacles. We lay out some of these obstacles in the form of real life problems, and we break down these obstacles using real life solutions. But our understanding of the problems and the solutions are markedly different. That's the fun part. You may read this looking for confirmation of your way of looking at things. If you find that in here, you will have done so by also reading another way of looking at the same thing, and therein lies the purpose. We want this book to strengthen hope, in all of its forms, and give living examples of how differently-minded people can arrive at the same destination.

Chapter 1

Hope

Eric

So, what is hope, and where do you find it? All of us have obstacles, burdens, and troubles, and some of us are finding it harder and harder to cope. The past few years have seemed to emphasize less tolerance for those who need or want help or can't keep up. The rhetoric of this world has been that there is only alienation and despair left for those of us outside the winners' circle, and that limiting view has left many of us feeling hopeless. But there is good news in this nearly barren field. Hope can survive anywhere. I have seen in my clinical work more broken spirits than you can count. I have seen people who have hurt themselves and others beyond the imagination. I have seen people break down to the point of finding no words, or even tears, to be able to express their torment. Yet, I have seen so many of them transform over time, so many returning to previous, healthier lives, and some even creating new incredible lives for the first time. It all had to start with hope. Something had to change from "I can't" to "Maybe, just maybe, I can."

There are three, tiny English words that are some of the most powerful in the hope lexicon. I have used them all with clients in

1

trying to establish a sense of possibility. As both Anthony and I say throughout this book, the messages we send ourselves are the most powerful determinants of our story. We can tell ourselves to believe or disbelieve. We can make decisions to change or not. We can listen to our "tapes" (our deep-seeded messages or voices in our heads) or rewrite them. We determine that. We tell ourselves what to try, what to be open to, or what to ignore. Sometimes, those decisions can set things in motion beyond what we could imagine.

The first of the tiny words is "yet" This simple, add-on word changes everything from destiny to possibility in one simple utterance and it can truly change one's entire message from disparagement to hope. I can change "I can't fix it" to "I can't fix it, yet" without much difficulty at all, and this simple adjustment acknowledges both realities of where one is and where one wants to be. It suggests possibility, perseverance, and, of course, hope.

The other two words are equally simple, but together propose a powerful question. "Why" and "not," said alone, seem to be distrustful at best and negative at worst. Put them together, and they become hope in its basic form. Why not? Why not, indeed! About twenty years ago, I went through many life changes at once, and found myself with quite a number of negative feelings and consequences. I was feeling alone and isolated. While I had friends and family, parts of my life in those arenas and others were crumbling. While I tried to stabilize my life, I did attempt to turn to God. Despite my want, I continued to struggle, but my "tapes," anger, and cynicism brought out by life's events, kept a solid wall between me and any real possibility of a relationship with a Higher Power.

One day, when I was feeling particularly deflated and lost, I walked by a desert rose in the courtyard of my place of work. It was the lone potted plant in the courtyard of a treatment center. It was the same pathetic desert rose that had been there for a long time. It was a spindly and sickly plant, ravaged by aphids, poor sunlight, and lack of care. The dirt surrounding its roots had been used repeatedly as an ashtray for those hurrying by, rushing to take a last drag before getting inside the adjacent building. This desert rose was browner than green and was bent to the point of breaking.

Hope

But *this* desert rose, on *this* day, of all days, managed to muster the strength to push forth a weak, barely viable blossom. The small pink and red flower stood in marked contrast to the thorny, twisted stem. I stopped and marveled at the survival and perseverance of this seemingly doomed plant that refused to stop trying. And it occurred to me, as you might guess: Was this a sign? Was it meant for me to see and for me to interpret as a message? The obvious, practical answer was, and remains, that it was a random encounter. But I had not been able to connect to hope for some time. I had not been able to believe in anything . . . yet. So, the next question was what would drive me to hope from despair? The question was, "Why not?" Why couldn't it be a sign? There was nothing painted on the plant that read "This is not a sign," so perhaps it could be. Perhaps this plant was put in my line of sight so that I might see that patience and effort would eventually show me something beautiful.

I conjure that event and feeling often, as a way to continue to feel connected to hope and possibility. Just that question of "Why not?" allowed me to suspend the need for any confirmation and be open to hope's possibility. It started to spread into my life. About the same time, I started to adopt rainbows in much the same way. In Florida we have a lot of rainbows, and they've always seemed unique and beautiful to me. When I needed it most, I came to entertain the idea that when I saw one, perhaps it was meant for me to see. Why not? The feeling that I did not deserve the individual attention gave way to the idea that I did not deserve it . . . yet, and then that morphed into the "why not" scenario that gifted me with hope.

Today, when I see a rainbow, I have an inventory of reactions without fail. My first is that a rainbow is a beautiful manifestation of hope. The second is a realization that today, I don't need the signs from anywhere to know that I deserve hope in my future. Third is a deeper desire that someone else is seeing that rainbow, wondering if it's a sign for them. I always hope so.

Finding Hope in Hopelessness

There are clinical and scientific ways of establishing hope. One such method is through a therapeutic intervention called Motivational Interviewing.[1]

In this brief process, the therapist asks the client to measure their desire and their belief in their ability to change. Additionally, the therapist provides clinical data to the client about situation and the commonalities the client shares with other individuals. In so doing, the client is reminded that they are normal human beings with normal problems to manage and are additionally reminded that change will take motivation and the belief in something different. Once those clinical agreements are established, one has the underpinnings of what I would call hope.

Trust in a therapist is key to success in therapy. It is clinically established that there is a direct link between the basic relationship of a client and therapist and the outcome of therapy.[2]

In simplest terms, if you believe that therapists can help, they are more likely to be able to help. Establish trust, and you establish hope. Medical advances in the treatment of depression, anxiety, and brain diseases give hope beyond what therapy can give. They give tangible light at the end of the tunnel for an ever-widening array of difficult situations. There are so many possibilities that simply did not exist when I first started in this business of helping others. Tomorrow will undoubtedly bring more.

I don't think it's trite to look for hope in nature or in human nature either, for that matter. I remember as a child thumbing through a magazine and seeing pictures of a war. Given my age, I suppose it was either Vietnam or perhaps a Middle Eastern conflict, I don't know for sure. But I vividly remember the photograph of a serviceman, atop a bullet and bomb-riddled building, crouched and battle ready. It must have been Christmastime, for a few feet from him was a small tree, cut and stuck in a crack in the concrete, and decorated with paper ornaments. That tree, contrasting all

1. Hartney, "Motivational Interviewing," sec 3.

2. Ardito and Rabellino, "Therapeutic Alliance and Outcome of Psychotherapy," 1.

around it, was as big a sign as if it were made of neon lights. That image still reminds me today that hope lives everywhere.

Anthony

There is another three-letter word that on its face may not have much significance; however, when two more words follow, it has tremendous significance! The first word is "but," and the other two words are "the Lord." When these three words, "but the Lord," travel together, anything life throws at us is possible to overcome.

In June of 2015, I had the great pleasure of meeting Dr. Ben Carson. At a later date, on September 14, 2021, I witnessed his presentation at an American Association of Christian Counselors (AACC) gathering in Orlando, Florida, entitled, "Way Maker World Conference for Mental Health and Ministry Professionals." There, Dr. Carson shared an incredibly powerful story of a mother and father who brought in their four year old son with a terminal, malignant brain-stem cancer. At that time, Dr. Carson was the Director of Pediatric Neurosurgery at the Johns Hopkins Children's Center. These parents had already been told by many other doctors to take their son home and let him die in peace because there wasn't anything more that could be done to save his life.

Each time Dr. Carson informed the parents that there was absolutely nothing he or anyone else could do, the parents responded, "But the Lord."

Dr. Carson was so impacted by the faith and hope demonstrated by these parents that he decided to do a biopsy. The results showed a high-grade glioma, a very malignant tumor. He went out to inform the parents that it was what they found, and again they responded, "But the Lord is going to heal our son." Dr. Carson said that he had never seen people with faith like this. He fully expected that the boy would deteriorate over the next few days and pass away, but instead, the boy began to look better. To Dr. Carson's shock and surprise at the boy's improvement, he ordered another scan. The tumor was still there, but Dr. Carson noticed that there was a small spot that was not attached directly to the brain stem.

He said the nature of the tumor had completely changed, and he realized the tumor was compressed against the brain stem! Dr. Carson decided to operate again. That boy walked out of the hospital, and today he's a minister! Dr. Carson went on to say that up until that point he always thought he was saving people, but he realized that day that God was the one who was saving people. Dr. Carson said from that point on, all kinds of miraculous things started to happen with his patients, and this is how he became the man of faith that he is today.

I find it interesting that one of Miriam Webster's definitions of hope is, "A desire accompanied by expectation of or belief in fulfillment."[3] In the New Testament book of Hebrews, verse 11:1 (NIV) says, *"Now faith is the assurance of things hoped for, the conviction of things not seen."* Different word choices from completely different mindsets, yet they arrive at a similar place.

Let's look at what the author of most of the New Testament, the apostle Paul, profoundly wrote in 2 Corinthians 4:18 (NIV), *"So we fix our eyes not on what is seen, but on what is unseen, since what is seen is temporary, but what is unseen is eternal."* This really hits home because for most of my life I have focused on the problems which did, in fact, turn out to be temporary. The problems in the majority of cases had much to do with me and those around me. These days, my focus is primarily on the solution, which is God who is eternal. So, in a world where so much emphasis is placed on the things we can see and touch, you may want to take a step back and begin to redirect the focus on the things unseen—faith and hope.

Eric

Hope is critical to change. It is the belief that a future different from the present is possible. Therapeutic intervention or divine intervention, the goal is the same. In therapy people often reference Pandora's Box as a way of saying, "I am afraid of what is inside

3. "Hope."

of me." To that I have come to be of a different mind. I feel, clinically and otherwise, that what is inside is the potential for understanding. Understanding what drives us may not be essential, but understanding where we came from can help us to know where we need to go. Remember the story of Pandora's Box. The last item in Pandora's Box was Hope.[4] When all else is gone, Hope remains.

Anthony

As Eric and I collaborate on this book, there are just three days left in 2021. As you probably know firsthand, this has been another extremely difficult year. At a time of great sorrow, despair, and even the loss of hope, I would be remiss in writing about hope and not referencing this verse from the first half of Hebrews 6:19 (NIV), *"We have this hope as an anchor for the soul, firm and secure."* An anchor keeps the boat or ship stable in a storm. An anchor keeps the vessel from drifting. What is your anchor for life's storms?

I know the pain of being hopeless all too well. I have also witnessed hopelessness countless times on the faces of the clients who enter our Faith in Recovery program at Banyan Treatment Centers. More often than not, however, something truly amazing happens. Newly planted seeds of hope, carefully positioned in a heavy heart, begin to grow and eventually blossom, creating a stunning metamorphosis like that of a caterpillar into a beautiful, free butterfly. This may sound overly dramatic, but it's actually true. I can't think of a better way to describe it. Don't lose hope simply because you cannot see what God is doing in your life. In His perfect timing, it will all make perfect sense.

4. Fraser, "Hope: A Foundation," para. 3.

Chapter 2

Commonalities

Eric

WHY DO WE THINK this book is useful in its style? In other words, is there a point to doing this book together, Anthony and I? After all, if there is so much to be gained from biblical messaging and pastoral counseling, or from psychotherapy and secular intervention, why not write separate books? Truthfully, it might be less confusing to some. It also might be easier for people to read what is familiar to them and relate to what is most relatable.

There were two reasons I think we wanted to do this. First, we are friends. We wanted to do something together that was fun, collaborative, and in keeping with both of our personalities. We both like to write sometimes, and we both like to help people. We thought it might be interesting to see what we came up with. Second, we wanted to show that it could be done. We were not trying to solve every problem, but we wanted to show others that we don't have to agree, or look at the world in the same way, to produce something useful together. In brief examples, both the Harvard

Business Review[1] and Now[2] point to scientific research on diversity, and the conclusion is clear. Diverse groups with different ways of thinking produce better products.

Anthony and I definitely don't agree on a lot of things, and our differences are reflected in many ways. He has a pit-bull; I have a dachshund. He lives near the ocean; I live in suburbia. Anthony is a devout man of faith; I have my doubts. But in today's world we often hear of confirmation bias, where people seek out ideas that match their own to affirm their righteousness, rather than entertain opposing views, in order to challenge their assumptions. The result is division and siloed thinking, partisanship, and discord. I don't believe what Anthony believes, but I have not lived Anthony's life. Anthony has helped people. I have seen that firsthand. He has helped me.

We come together because we focus on commonality. We compromise and we negotiate. Don't confuse commonality with similarity. We are not the same. We don't think or act the same. We do have commonalities. We do have things that we can agree on. That's the part we start with. There is an age-old debate as to whether or not science and religion can co-exist, and I am not qualified to weigh in on such an academic debate. I do believe, however, that the answer may be in the details of life on the ground level. The answer may be found where we just get up each day and go to work, trying to do our best to do the next right thing. I use science every day. I believe in it. I was taught in school that everything is electrical, mathematical, and predictable. However, I also listened when someone said that Einstein only had theories, and that we had never seen the end of an infinite number. I learned in school that there are things I don't and perhaps can't understand. I do not see a reason to doubt that there are things that I don't know on such a profound level as that which is spiritual, when there are things I don't know about, such as, how a lightbulb works or a car runs. Anthony can tell you why he believes faith heals. I can tell

1. Rock and Grant, "Why Diverse Teams Are Smarter," para. 3.

2. Gifford, et al, "The Intersection of Technology, Innovation and Creativity," para. 1.

you what I know about why the brain responds the way it does. Neither one of us knows that we are right; we just both believe we can help. We want to help people see hope.

Anthony

Ronald Reagan, who in my opinion was an amazing leader and communicator, had the ability to work together with those who disagreed with him and were completely on opposite sides of the spectrum. This is one of our former President Reagan's many great quotes: "*The person who agrees with you 80 percent of the time is a friend and an ally—not a 20 percent traitor.*" What a difference forty-something years can make! These days the battle lines are drawn on just about everything imaginable. Any trace of commonality is replaced with canceling any person who doesn't agree with you. "Shut up and listen!" is an ever-growing theme. "Crush anyone who doesn't conform to your views—yeah that will teach them!"

In some circles in today's world, thinking outside the box is absurd, but others say to think outside the box is to think creatively. "*Thinking outside the box is more than just a business cliché. It means approaching problems in new, innovative ways, conceptualizing problems differently, and understanding your position in relation to any particular situation in a way you'd never thought of before.*"[3]

"This phrase, incidentally, is thought to be connected to the nine-dot puzzle, first recorded in 1914 in Sam Lloyd's *Cyclopedia of Puzzles*. Perhaps you've seen this puzzle before where your task is to link all 9 dots using four straight lines or less, without lifting the pen. The solution? Think outside the box! This puzzle and its accompanying phrase were adopted by consultants in the 1970's and 1980's and were spread to corporations around the world."[4]

As Eric mentioned, we do not always agree on things, but disagreement doesn't divide us. I believe in my heart of hearts, our agreeing to disagree makes us stronger. Better solutions emerge!

3. Wax, "11-ways," para. 1.
4. Davis, "Jargon Genesis: Think," para. 3.

The foundation of this kind of relationship has to be respect for the other person's opinions. Upon experiencing a bird's eye view of how Eric and our CEO Joe Tuttle have built this incredible company that has positively impacted thousands of lives, I have tremendous respect for both Eric Oakes and Joe Tuttle. They are incredibly intelligent, gifted, and focused leaders. More importantly, they are incredibly good human beings. The kind of success they have attained building this company doesn't happen by chance. In fact, it rarely happens at all in the industry. I believe their success has to do with their taking a leap of faith to become one of the few substance-abuse and mental health organizations in the country to have a comprehensive faith-based program.

We recently expanded our faith-based services into all Banyan centers across the country at all levels of care. Although I, myself, am blessed to head this up, I truly didn't realize the significance of this national expansion until after updating my LinkedIn information. LinkedIn automatically sends out updated profile information to all connections on the platform. As a result, I was quickly flooded with responses, not just nationally, but globally! LinkedIn members responded with this sentiment: So many places are removing God, but you guys are embracing God, and this has given me a new sense of hope!

I know that God doesn't need me or Banyan to extend His reach, but I also know that He works through people. He will use rescued people to help rescue others who are hurting. He has done it throughout the Bible with the most unlikely of characters. So maybe God is using Eric and me now to encourage people in an extraordinarily divisive time to take a step back and listen to the opinions of others. Who knows? You may suddenly realize that you agree with more of this approach than you ever thought you would, and you may begin the journey of working together with those you disagree with to make a difference in people's lives, people who may be in desperate need of hope.

Eric

One last thing before a greater discussion. We are going to be look-ing for hope in real life, and we are going to find it hidden behind obstacles. One of those obstacles, we have just outlined. That is the process of establishing a line of communication. We cannot have a discussion here if one of us refuses to participate. So, a question emerges: What if the heels are so dug in, on either side, that discus-sion feels impossible?

I am going to only guess that Anthony would say that a dis-cussion with God would then be in order because He is always listening. I would say that some might find this unsatisfactory. To those people, I would suggest that this process might be a bit like a knot in a shoelace or a string. It is easy to give up when the knot seems to just get tighter the harder you try to work it free. But the fact is, the knot is not permanently stuck. If you have patience, massage it, try different angles, and use different resources. Even-tually some part of that knot will begin to give, and that is the first sign of hope. You might need to set it aside for a while because frustration builds. Come back later. You may need to try prying it open with a tool or asking for someone else's help, but eventually, almost all knots can be undone.

Anthony

"Two are better than one because they have a good return for their labor." Ecclesiastes 4:9 (NIV) When individuals work together, they can double their strength and get much more done as a team. They also reap the value of having worked in unison, thus creat-ing harmony instead of disorder. Working as one people begins with the efforts of each person, as they work with another person.[5] Solomon, the writer of Ecclesiastes, speaks of the advantages of fellowship, partnerships, self-control, and mutual encouragement between two people. "Two are better than one," he writes, "because they have a good return for their labor."

5. Robinson, "Ecclesiastes 4:9," last para.

Our God is a relational God, and He has made us to be part of a family and members of society. As referenced above, we can see a contrast between those whose lives are motivated by the futility of envy or isolated by selfish greed and inappropriate incentives, as opposed to the comfort, help, encouragement, and reward which is gained in trusted friendships or a reliable partner in times of need.[6]

In the world today, and especially with those suffering with mental health disorders and addiction, there are many people who are suffering and are desperate for hope. When we set our differences of opinion aside, we give them a fighting chance. To those who are suffering, we provide more emotional tools to deal with what life to throws at them. Together we can impact those who are in great need of hope. They deserve this chance; they deserve the opportunity to overcome adversity and to find hope in their hopelessness.

6. "What Does Ecclesiastes Mean?" para. 5–6.

Chapter 3

Shame

Anthony

You may have heard it said, "Shame on you!" or how about this beauty—"You should be ashamed of yourself!" Shame typically comes up when you look inward with a critical eye and evaluate yourself harshly, often for things over which you have little control. This negative self-evaluation often has its roots in messages you've received from others, especially during your childhood. When parents or teachers criticized you, rather than calling to your attention any poor behavior choices you may have made, they planted the seed of shame.

Shame centers on your very identity as a person, and it becomes particularly toxic when it starts to impact your sense of self. Toxic shame opens the door to anger, self-disgust, and other less-than-desirable feelings. It can make you feel small and worthless. It can trickle into your inner dialogue like a poison, locking you into a painful loop of negative self-talk.

"When toxic shame lingers without resolution, the desire to hide from it or escape can lead to potentially harmful behaviors like substance misuse or self-harm."[1] Did you catch that? Negative self-talk can lead to negative self-harm and harmful behaviors. So why would we continue to operate in shame and beat ourselves up with our own thoughts and words? Easier said than done; similar to the question you may have heard such as, "Why don't you just stop drinking?" At face value it's a completely logical question. Something is destroying you, yet you continue to allow it to be part of your life. It seems basic enough as if we can simply turn it off like a light switch. Well, not exactly that easy.

We are introduced to shame very early in Scripture in Genesis 3. You may have heard the story. The serpent deceived Eve, and both she and Adam ate from the only tree that God told them not to eat from—the tree of the knowledge of good and evil. What happens next is how it relates to the topic of shame. What's interesting is that in Genesis 2:25 (NIV), *"Adam and his wife were both naked, and they felt no shame."*

In the next chapter things take quite a turn for the worse. Genesis 3:8–10 (NIV) says, *"Then the man and his wife heard the sound of the Lord God as he was walking in the garden in the cool of the day, and they hid from the Lord God among the trees of the garden. But the Lord God called to the man, 'Where are you?'"* Adam answered, *"I heard you in the garden, and I was afraid because I was naked; so I hid."* So, why the dramatic change of heart? The only thing that changed from not being ashamed in Genesis 2:25 to being afraid and hiding from God was sin.

How does this relate to us today in our own lives? Let's start with the deception from our own desires, the disobedience to God. Genesis 3:6 (NIV) says, *"When the woman saw that the fruit of the tree was good for food and pleasing to the eye, and also desirable, she took some and ate it."* James 1:13–15 (NIV) tells us, *"When tempted, no one should say, 'God is tempting me.' For God cannot be tempted by evil, nor does he tempt anyone; but each person is tempted when they are dragged away by their own evil desire and enticed. Then, after desire has conceived, it gives birth to sin; and sin, when it is full-grown, gives birth to death."* So, disobedience to God is quickly

1. Raypole, "Where Toxic Shame Comes From," para.4.

followed by hiding from God. Finally comes the shame and then the consequences which are found in Genesis 3:16–19 (NIV).

So, if you are more analytical, this calculus may be a more concise way to present it:

Deception + Desire + Disobedience = Shame and Consequences. Can I get a witness? Can I get an amen? (For the record that was another attempt of mine at some humor on not the most pleasant of topics. Trust me; my jokes only get better as we move forward in the book.)

Let's move on and make it more personal. Maybe you have experienced shame or are experiencing it right now. Shame can be very difficult to deal with and in many cases it's quite demoralizing. Shame is particularly relevant with those struggling with addiction and or mental health disorders. You may find yourself not only isolating from people but also hiding from God. I know I did. You may believe that God exists, yet you are living outside His will. Maybe anger wells up in you at the mention of His name. You may have professed the words, "Thy will be done," but only with empty words and not from the heart. Do you realize that God hears all your words?

From a faith perspective, the issue of shame can keep us from the deeper relationship that God desires to have with us. We may think we are too far gone and God has written us off. We may think the hurt we have caused our families is beyond God's forgiveness. I want to encourage you to please resist the impulse to hide from God. There is still hope in what may feel like a hopeless situation. He's our father through Christ and has an unconditional love for us. He has not given up on you as He didn't give up on me, even though I gave Him many reasons to do just that! He still has a plan for your life; great purpose can emerge from the pain you've experienced. God is in the business of restoring lives, and it's not too late for you to stop hiding in shame. Allow Him to restore you into the person He has created you to be. John 1:12 (NIV) tells us, *"Yet to all who did receive him, to those who believed in his name, he gave the right to become children of God."*

We want our true identity to be *not* the persons we were when we were in active addiction or when we were completely broken in spirit, hurting people from our own hurt. A child of God is the identity that He desires for all of us, and He accomplished this through Christ Jesus.

Eric

John Bradshaw was the pre-eminent thought leader on shame in popular culture of the 1990s. His writing was my truth, as he captured the essence of shame in a way that was personal to me. It was he who stated with emphasis the profoundest definition of what Anthony correctly labeled toxic shame. Bradshaw contends that while "guilt" is defined by feeling bad for having *made* a mistake, "shame" is characterized by feeling bad for *being* a mistake.[2] Think about that. You didn't make a mistake; you *are* the mistake! You, shame tells you, are not worthy of anything at all. Not decency, not respect, not happiness, and surely not love, because you aren't really even supposed to exist. You are a mistake. You are all wrong. All of you is broken.

In the recent past, I have heard the emergence of a new term for what holds the same message. Actress Viola Davis spoke at a recent awards ceremony of her self-described Imposter Syndrome.[3] She explained that beneath her glamorous and seemingly successful exterior, her message to herself, her belief, is that she is an actress, fooling others into thinking she is something she is not, and that if we knew her truths, we would know how unworthy she is.

I have spoken several times of my "tapes" that play in my head. It took me years to identify what they were saying. I always knew the tapes were playing, but they were always muffled and unclear. I knew they contributed to my unhealthy feelings, but I wasn't sure how. One day, seemingly out of nowhere, the tapes played clear as day. They told me, "Eric, even your name is an embarrassment.

---

2. Bradshaw, *Healing the Shame That Binds You.*, 21–45, 223–235.

3. Taylor, "Oscar-winning actress Viola Davis," para. 1–2.

Everything about you is a fraud. Everyone can see the real you, so why do you even pretend? Stop Trying. You are exposed. Everyone knows you are worthless." My shame was so deep, that I shamed myself for pretending to be a successful human being. My shame was so deep, that I constantly told myself that it was only a matter of time before my prophecy was fulfilled, and my world of lies would collapse, and I would take my rightful place at the bottom of the pile of the pitiful and scorned.

Where did these tapes come from? I am not sure. As Anthony mentioned earlier, my father used to wield the exact phrases, "I am ashamed of you!" and "You should be ashamed of yourself!" That wasn't always the message, but it certainly was in his repertoire. Why does it matter? I am not sure it does. I can surmise that peers and popular culture gave me messages that I internalized as well. There is certainly a plethora of messaging out there—marketing, advertising, and media, that tell you that you are nothing if you are not something they want you to be, so I would guess that I was susceptible to some of that messaging perhaps more than others. I don't care. I think the message I would want others to hear is that the messages you send yourself can be changed. You can change the tapes. You may not be able to erase them, but you can record over them with a different message. As Anthony said that self-talk could lead to self-harm, so then can self-talk lead to self-love?

So here is the true secret about shame. It doesn't have to be a secret. You know what I am going to say next: You can tell on yourself! If you do, you will discover just how not alone you are. Everyone has shame. Everyone has some messages in their head that tell them they have a secret they shouldn't share about their shortcomings. In my job I am often called to speak in front of large groups. It is not uncommon for me to talk to dozens or hundreds of people. Over the years, I slowly began to tell on myself. Today, it is not unusual for me to express that I am nervous, or intimidated, or that I feel unworthy. I have even told groups exactly what my tapes say. I have told them that I feared that if I kept speaking, they would figure out that I didn't know what I was talking about. As it happened, no one has ever used it against me.

Over the years, I have worked with clients on a cognitive exercise to change their self-narrative, or the unconscious story they tell themselves about why they are the way they are. I have asked them to draw a tree with a big trunk, with a handful of branches, and a handful of deep roots. Then I have asked them to label the branches with some of the things in their lives they would like to change. Over the coming sessions, we then worked to identify the roots that feed those branches, labeling what some of the causes were for the issues the client was hoping to change. So often, the causes, or roots, got labeled as messages from the self, in one form or another, that the client felt in some way, deserving of the negative things in their lives, and unworthy of a better outcome. This is shame. I have seen people cry as they realize the fundamental falsehood of these shame messages. I have seen them gain pride and confidence as they start to send new, healthier roots into the soil. This is how shame turns to hope.

Change your "tapes." No one is a mistake. Everyone makes mistakes. Everyone has shame. No one deserves it. As before mentioned by Bradshaw, this is not guilt. Guilt has logic to it. This is not humility. Humility is about keeping self-importance in check and realizing that you are not the center of the universe. Shame to me is like your appendix; it probably used to help somehow, but we don't need it anymore.

Anthony

Two points that Eric makes really hit home with me and hopefully will with you as well.

"You can change the 'tapes.' You may not be able to erase the 'tapes,' but you can record over them with a different message." Unfortunately, replaying those tapes continuously is not uncommon. I lived in that devastating mindset for the next seven years. I would never leave home without them, so to speak.

I'm sure that at one time or another you have watched a really horrible movie. It may have even been recommended by a friend. I actually watched one of those horrible movies last night that was recommended by many people over a period of years. I had the luxury of turning it off about halfway through, so I only wasted about an hour on it. When life happens, we often can't or won't turn off the horrible movie—quite the contrary; we keep hitting the play button. My reward for playing those horrible tapes for seven years was complete and utter misery, and that's just scratching the surface! I was trying to change the past, but we simply cannot change the past; we can only learn from it and grow from it.

The other excellent point Eric made is this: "So here is the true secret about shame. It doesn't have to be a secret." Those are words that I can truly relate to in my own journey—words that can profoundly impact lives. If I had heard those words in 2005 and actually applied them to my situation, I would have avoided tremendous pain and suffering. If you are in the darkness of shame, you don't have to wait seven years or continue to live in the torment of shame for even the next seven minutes. Give this some serious thought.

Maybe you are pondering this question: How can I truly overcome shame? It may feel as if it's a part of who you are. It's not! Consider this approach: face it head on! Begin to be transparent and open with past mistakes and poor choices. Take ownership of them and move on. Life is not a dress rehearsal; it's moving, and at times it seems to be moving at warp speeds.

There is a beautiful life out there waiting for you. Allow God to turn your shame and pain into something which will empower and encourage others facing similar challenges. You may even find that in the process of encouraging others, you too are becoming a recipient of that encouragement.

One final point and the most important one: I mentioned that we cannot change the past; we can only learn and grow from it. However, there *is* someone who can change our past. God can change it by forgiving us of all sins and horrible choices. Hebrews 8:12 tells us, *"For I will forgive their wickedness and will remember their sins no more."* The promised assurance of God's forgiveness through The Lord Jesus Christ is not simply a game changer. It is an eternity changer! If you are looking to find hope in hopelessness, it doesn't get more hopeful than that.

Eric

We are making two assumptions in this entry. First is that this concept of shame is important because it is harmful. Some will make an argument that it's necessary, and, as Anthony elucidates from the biblical references, it's an ancient concept. I am not sure I fully comprehend all of Anthony's points, as I am not sure I have ever fully understood how to treat God as a being who actively intervenes in my individual life. However, the problem with shame is that it actually keeps you from growth, health, and happiness. One definition is that you are actually unworthy to receive those things. Shame can keep you from feeling the confidence and safety you need to address other things in your life, making it doubly destructive.

The second assumption is that we see hope shine through when we tackle these things that challenge us, even when change takes work. It might be easy for some, and hard for others, but it is work just the same. The good news is that lots of professional people who are really good at this stuff can help. If we are willing to work on ourselves just a little, there is, once again, real hope.

Chapter 4

Substance Use

Eric

I HAVE SPENT THE better part of my professional career helping individuals find alternatives to a life of substance-seeking and substance-abuse. It is hard to fit what I have experienced into a couple of pages. Over the past thirty-five years, I have seen significant shifts in science, culture, and attitudes. I have witnessed many triumphs, and, most unfortunately, many deaths. I don't think I have to argue that drugs are a problem sometimes, and that some drugs can kill people. I don't think I have to argue that there are components that compel people to label addiction as a disease. What I do wonder about, is the rest of it.

Labeling addiction as a disease seems to me a bit simplistic and reductionistic, not because I don't think that is true, but because I don't think it says all there is to say. It seems to take a drug, make it into a case for all other drugs, express it all in a vacuum, and draw conclusions that drugs and addictions go hand-in-hand. Don't misunderstand, I run treatment centers because I know drug use can and does destroy lives, relationships, jobs, families, and everything else. I know that without careful care, people who try to quit drugs like alcohol and benzodiazepines are vulnerable to deadly seizures. I believe with all my heart that many people need to have training to learn new ways of living after removing drugs from their system. I have seen the evidence that I believe shows the brain becomes diseased. But I have also concluded that people are dying while the debate rages on.

But the simplification part is that I don't think most people think about what goes into the use in the first place. There are a lot of us who use drugs to feel good or to feel better. There are a lot of us who use drugs because the doctor told us to. We use drugs to kill pain or to have fun. There are a lot of us who use drugs because we are searching for something on a spiritual level. Are all of us abusing the drugs? No, of course not. Are all of us damaged by the use? No, of course not. Are many of us kept from reaching our potential because we use too many drugs too often? Maybe. Probably. Yes. Many of us find ourselves in complex situations, and while the start may be to stop taking a drug, the situations that led to the use have to be addressed in proper context.

The reductionistic part is that we leave out issues of gambling, sex, food, and shopping. So many are reluctant to call "addiction" to these things real issues, relegating them to issues of character and self-control. Yet, I have known so many who have lost so much, as more and more research seems to be supporting the idea that these are real problems hurting real folks.

Where do people lose hope? People lose hope when there is no conceivable way out. The stories in treatment are endless of people who arrived at a place in their lives where they continued to use drugs or alcohol even though they knew that it would likely result in death because it no longer seemed to matter, and it no longer seemed to be possible to change. Tragically, many continue along this self-fulfilling path. Yet, many are willing to grasp at any sign of hope, sometimes nothing more than a smile or a handshake from another, and are willing to work their way back to meaning, purpose, and even joy.

There is no doubt that all drugs impact brain function. All drugs impact our brains differently. Some drugs are more damaging to the body than others. If you have any doubt as to the science, Dr. Nora Volkow, the Director of the National Institute of Drug Abuse, has researched, published, and spoken extensively on ground-breaking findings in the brain.[1] If you have any doubt as to the social and scientific complexity of addiction, Dr. Tom Horvath has written extensively on the subject.[2] Each in their own right have elevated the science of the field beyond measure and have driven the dialogue forward.

Treatment methods for misuse, abuse, and addiction have evolved in recent years. When I first began in addiction treatment, most treatment was the same. Anyone who sought help went into an inpatient hospital and received cognitive or behavioral therapies, and then was introduced to a 12-step program of recovery. Now, with scientific advancement, there are myriad options at an inpatient and outpatient level for treatment, including many alternatives to 12-step programs. At Banyan Treatment Centers, we have striven to adopt meaningful and effective treatments that allow us to treat the whole person in the way that fits the need. We offer everything from intensive inpatient care to telehealth outpatient sessions, and treat people with medicines, talk therapies, and experiential therapies. Because we believe that addiction does not happen in a vacuum, we treat families as well.

There is still a tendency to make drug use and abuse a moral problem or a willpower problem. While I would venture a guess that many of us have family members who drink too much, have been arrested for drug possession, or have even ended up hospitalized, we still would prefer to relegate the issue to some other group of people. Despite the fact that it's already in our houses or in our families, we work to try to keep it a secret, and are ashamed that we don't have the moral fortitude to save ourselves. Denial is a well-established concept of ignoring or being unable to see the truth in our lives. Denial is called a defense mechanism because it protects us from pain. It is a good thing from time to time. Sometimes, however, denial becomes harmful when it keeps us from seeing

1. Volkow, *National Institute on Drug Abuse*, para. 1–2.
2. Horvath, *Practical Recovery*, para. 1.

how our pain is self-inflicted. That is not a statement of blame; that is an assertion that we know we are hurting ourselves when we hit our thumb with a hammer, but do we know it when we are using more pills than we were prescribed?

Some years ago, I decided to remove alcohol use from the equation of my life. I have always been a bit compulsive. Once I start something, I don't always moderate well. I don't have one piece of cake. I don't do a little yardwork. I eat cake until it comes out of my pores, and I do yardwork until I am near heat exhaustion. I have never been someone who understood the notion of a glass of wine or a beer. If I was going to drink, I was going to drink until I was done drinking. I stated elsewhere that, as a younger person, I had used substances to alter my state as an escape. I also stated that early on, a professional had suggested that I examine my use, and I declined. But eventually the message was clear. After using alcohol for decades, it had long outlived its benefits and had long ago moved into the cost category. Alcohol had too many times been what I was doing with my time, rather than something I did while doing something else. I went out to drink. I went home to drink. I drank to have fun. It was eventually going to consume me, and that eventuality was decidedly near. It was no longer fun; it was necessary.

The saying goes that substances make you give up everything for one thing, and sobriety is about giving up one thing to get everything. It's not an easy trade at the time, but it's a trade I would make any day. Every desire to have a beer with my friend or a toast with my family or a glass of wine at sunset is a fantasy to me. My reality, however, is never being afraid of stupid arguments, risky behavior, time wasted hungover, or having to be reminded of the night before.

So, hope enters here. The assertion is that drug use, once it evolves to where it is interfering with your life, job, relationships, may not be something you can control, regardless of willpower or desire. The use that has become misuse or even dependence may not be your fault. But you can take responsibility and you can decide for yourself what you want in life.

Today, I work next to people as colleagues who have been to the edge and back. Some of the smartest, bravest, and kindest people I know have a history that would make for a blockbuster of a horror movie. One of the best friends I have had in my life was a former priest who had burned down his own church in the middle of a drug-fueled psychosis. Another of my friends was a woman who used to pour herself a full tumbler of vodka every morning before heading off to work, to stop the shaking from the night before. Many have physical and mental scars. But these stories of perseverance are proof of survival in the extreme. So many more of us are just looking for something different. A new start or new possibilities. We don't have to wait for our brain to be diseased to know that our current behavior is not working for us. In working with clients, I've observed they often cannot imagine going into a social situation without being able to have a drink or two to take the edge off. Even more believe that without alcohol, they will no longer be the life of the party. Some just know if they can't get their drug, they are going to get real sick. But few can imagine waking up and starting every day with a clear head and a clear conscience.

Anthony

Eric's breakdown of this hotly debated topic is very much on point. It is our hope that it sparks a deeper conversation. We have referenced in other chapters how religion and politics can be divisive by their very nature. In the addiction industry, the disease or not disease debate could be equally as divisive. The battle lines have been drawn.

When you move beyond the clichés and strong emotions that are so often stirred up regarding substance use, what's most important often gets lost in the shuffle. What's most important is the fact that people are dying in record numbers as a result of addiction. Many are young people, intelligent people who lost their sense of purpose, and not long after that, they lost all hope. For Eric and me and all others who work in the substance abuse and mental health industry, these people are not simply statistics on a spreadsheet.

They are actual people whose families will never see them again or hear their voices again on this side of eternity.

CDC: Fentanyl overdoses are now the leading cause of death for Americans aged 18 to 45. According to the CDC, fentanyl overdoses have killed more people aged 18 to 45 since 2020 than COVID, car accidents, and even suicides.[3]

According to Dr. Nora Volkow, Director of the National Institute on Drug Abuse, increase in fentanyl deaths started to rise abruptly in 2016 and continued to increase sharply throughout 2020 and 2021(from an interview with 25 News). The country lost 37,208 people during 2020 and 41,587 people just this year (in 2021) between the ages of 18 and 45. Eric provides a reality check with this insight: "I don't think I have to argue that there are components that compel people to label addiction as a disease. What I do wonder about is the rest of it. Labeling addiction as a disease seems to me to be a bit simplistic and reductionistic, not because I don't think that is true, but because I don't think it says all there is to say." Eric goes on to write, "But I have also concluded that people are dying while the debate rages on."

I believe he's right; it doesn't say all there is to say on the topic. When you are talking about addiction and co-occurring mental health disorders, you are talking about the brain, the most complex organ that God created by far. When people in an out of this field start painting addiction with a broad brush, it opens the door for senseless arguments, and, yes, people are dying while the debate is raging on! Unfortunately, this may sound all too familiar. It plays out with many other topics where the debates are raging on while people are dying throughout the country. Whether it is homelessness, addiction, mental health, veteran care, or numerous other issues, it's worth considering applying what we are attempting to covey throughout the chapters of this book. It is our hope that it will save lives.

From the introduction: "The point of this book is to relate a conversation between two people who see things differently but are willing to talk about them." This concept wasn't that far-fetched

3. Naspretto, "CDC Fentanyl Overdoses," 1.

not too long ago, even in the world of politics and other debatable arenas. "Coming together is a beginning, staying together is progress, and working together is success."[4]

From a biblical perspective, addiction falls into the category of strongholds. Strongholds are spiritual, but they show up in our soul. Our soul is composed of our mind (thinking), emotions (feeling), and will (choosing). Just because a person is biblically literate doesn't exclude the potential for strongholds. Strongholds (lies) are much deeper than surface level, and often times we don't even know what we've agreed with as truth in our hearts. Once we come in agreement with a lie, our perception of ourselves, of God, and of others gets tainted. Depending on the information we are digesting, this can be extremely toxic.[5]

I have heard this countless times from our clients at Banyan Treatment Centers and many others in recovery: "I had a relationship with God and would pray, etc., but as soon as I started using drugs, it was as if a wall came up between God and me."

So, what are these walls so many speak of and this distance from God upon active addiction? Well, I don't want to paint with a broad brush here, especially since I just mentioned above how we shouldn't paint with a broad brush on this topic; however, I will say this: God doesn't leave us or forsake us. We leave Him. Our sin and bad choices separate us from Him, as was referenced in the Shame chapter regarding Adam who experienced shame and began hiding from God right after the disobedience to God.

Oh, you may know the drill; maybe it shows up in your life this way: How can I pray after what I did last? I can't go to church after what I was thinking all day. God isn't going to want to hear from me. Instead, try looking at it with this perspective: God already heard from you when you did or thought whatever it is that you are now hiding from Him. You are not going to surprise God with anything, so it makes sense to go to Him, ask for forgiveness and the strength to overcome the struggle, then move forward.

4. Dunne, "35 Best Teamwork Quotes," #4.
5. "Addiction is a Stronghold," para. 5.

First John 1:9 NKJV says, *"If we confess our sins, He is faithful and just to forgive us our sins and to cleanse us from all unrighteousness."*

You may be thinking if God already knows what I did, why would I have to confess it to Him? We come in agreement with Him as to what we did was wrong. We will also be less likely to continue on the path of repeating the same mistakes.

Eric

Anthony and I have worked together for years. I hired him to work at Banyan many years ago with the idea that his perspective could be well-integrated into the mission and method of treatment in our facility. Anthony became the chaplain in our alternative, faith-based program and has been its champion, pioneer, and expert ever since. He has always walked a steady path of conviction. Yet, it has never been his assertion, nor our mission, that faith and prayer by themselves are all that is necessary. I have never asked Anthony how he makes sense of that issue in his heart, but his clients in his program, like every other program, receive therapies by licensed, masters-level clinicians, medical services by nurses and psychiatrists, and other services and therapies that are evidence based. The Faith in Recovery program is designed to provide a safe place to both explore a relationship with God and to use any and all strength and support that relationship might foster. It is an effective program, and Anthony does a great job leading it.

Addiction studies, scientists, and scholars in the industry are quite tolerant of the ambiguous relations between science and religion in drug treatment. There is likely no place where God and science so conspicuously share seats at the same table, sometimes vying to dominate, sometimes opting for something less dramatic, but nonetheless not wholly without tension. In 1902, William James, one of the fathers of modern psychology, philosophy, and addiction study, published one of the most famous works in our industry. *The Varieties of Religious Experience* pragmatically explored various relationships with God and became the basis for the concept of Higher Power in the 12-step programs still used today.

His thoughts created a path for people to look at possible practical use of the belief in something bigger than themselves. This is important because it laid the groundwork for application of faith to a real life scenario of recovery, using measured and meaningful steps. Given the writing of James Williams and the importance of 12-step programs in recovery for so many people, it is not such a leap that Anthony's program simply extends a step further and explains why it is logical for me to consider it a practical service option in our array of programming.[6]

Anthony

At Banyan Treatment Centers we are truly blessed with a wide range of treatment models from veterans in recovery programming, an array of clinical approaches, 12-step programming, mental health services, eating disorder programming, and faith-based programming. As Eric eloquently wrote above, our Faith in Recovery program is an integration of faith-based and clinical programming. This combined approach works extremely well. We meet clients right where they are on their spiritual journey. Over the years, those from all faith backgrounds or no faith background at all have chosen to attend and have completed the Faith in Recovery program. We are equally blessed at Banyan with top leadership and talented professionals at many levels throughout the organization.

One of the staples of the vast majority of substance abuse centers is the 12-step program. Historians have traced the genesis of the 12-step program in Alcoholics Anonymous back to the Oxford Group, an evangelistic movement from the early 1900s. Dr. Frank Buchman, a Lutheran minister from Pennsylvania Dutch heritage, was the founder of the Oxford Group. Dr. Buchman experienced a spiritual transformation in 1908 as he visited a small church in Cumberland. Envisioning the suffering face of the crucified Christ, he realized how his resentments had separated himself

6. Sheldon, "Belief Beyond Sobriety," (text below video), para. 1.

from God's unconditional love. He surrendered his will and will-fulness to God and began to share his experience with others. His work and an eventual following grew, with groups springing up at Oxford, Princeton, Yale, Harvard, Williams, Smith, and Vassar. Outreach was conducted through house meetings, and members were encouraged to find and work with people who suffered from problems similar to their own.

Bill Wilson, one of the co-founders of Alcoholics Anonymous, traced his journey to sobriety through the Oxford Group. In the subsequent development of Alcoholics Anonymous, Bill Wilson eventually distanced himself from the Oxford Group in order to reach out to Catholics and other groups who were uncomfortable with the evangelical emphasis. However, many of the traditions of the Oxford Group continue in the A.A. approach, and the Bible remains a foundation for recovery for many of those in A.A. and other 12-step groups.[7]

So, we see that the terminology has changed to not exclude those in need of help due to their denomination or those with no religious affiliation at all which, I believe, makes good sense. The core of this fellowship and the big book that has helped countless alcoholics and addicts over the years has its origins that lead straight back to the Bible, the biggest of books!

7. "The Bible and the 12 Steps," sec. 1.

Chapter 5

Forgiveness

Anthony

WHY ARE MANY OF us so reluctant to forgive those who have hurt or wronged us? Forgiveness is one of the core tenants of the Christian faith. Sure, we may have said the Lord's Prayer count-less times, but do we really mean what we ask God to do in that prayer—to forgive us as we forgive others?

Because I didn't apply forgiveness during a very difficult time of my life, the resentments culminated into what turned out to be the worst period of my life. My inability to forgive was the absolute root cause of major destruction in my own life.

What seems to take place many times is, we think in some distorted way that we are getting back at the person who caused us pain. We mistakenly think that we are achieving some sort of retribution while we remain in our corner, or more accurately, in our misery. You may have heard this or have said it yourself, "They don't deserve my forgiveness." News flash. Forgiveness is not for the other person; it's for us!

What is forgiveness? According to the American Psychological Association, forgiveness is the mental and/or spiritual process of ceasing to feel resentment, indignation, or anger against another person for a perceived offense, difference, or mistake, or ceasing to demand punishment or restitution. Forgiveness is choosing to stop feeding the anger and resentment toward the person who hurt you but letting out your hurt in a positive way.[1] Did you catch that part? "Forgiveness is the mental and/or spiritual process . . ."

Let's continue by looking at it from a spiritual perspective since that is what my sections are about. The New Testament book of Romans has been called the jewel of the Bible. It's truly a profound book that Paul wrote to the church in Rome. *"Do not be overcome by evil, but overcome evil with good."* (Romans 12:21 NIV)

Let's go back to the above reference. *"Forgiveness is choosing to stop feeding the anger and resentment toward the person who hurt you, but letting out your hurt in a positive way."*

Are you tracking with me here? Do you see the similarities? *"Letting your hurt out in a positive way . . ."* from the secular commentary, and from the biblical viewpoint, *"Overcome evil with good."* We arrive at the same place.

How do we work these things into our own lives? We choose to focus on how good could come out of the hurt. Look at the resentments you may be harboring against someone right now. What if you looked at it from that person's perspective? (Put the shoe on the other foot, so to speak.) This exercise may shed some light on what your part was in the conflict. I find that when I do this, forgiveness becomes easier; furthermore, the exercise provides me with some self- awareness.

I can't help thinking of the first part of what Jesus uttered from the cross, *"Father, forgive them, for they know not what they do."* Luke 23:34 (ESV) Jesus was interceding to God the Father on behalf of those who were mocking, humiliating, torturing, and crucifying Him. Maybe think of that the next time you are ready to harbor resentments against someone or to withhold forgiveness. I do this when I'm tempted to hold a grudge; I quickly realize that there is no comparison at any level to what I'm going through and to what Christ endured!

1. "What is Forgiveness?" para. 5.

One more passage from Romans, and this one literally played a major role in my being able to forgive someone who really caused me tremendous pain, loss, and anger: *"Never pay back evil with more evil. Do things in such a way that everyone can see you are honorable. Do all that you can to live in peace with everyone. Dear friends, never take revenge. Leave that to the righteous anger of God." Romans 12:17–19 (NLT)*

Thankfully, I have never been struck by lightning, but while reading this passage and dealing with major resentments, this verse hit me like a lightning bolt! I reread it numerous times before taking a leap of faith and applying the verse to my own desperate situation. I decided to make a real effort to put this verse into practice. No longer were these just words on a page; I wholeheartedly began to live by these words! This is the essence of how God transforms our hearts. We begin to surrender our will and ways to His will and ways. To God be all the glory.

Eric

The title of this chapter probably ought to be different. Forgiveness is a positive, noble, and freeing event. It is not then, forgiveness that is an obstacle to hope, but rather the lack thereof. It is a struggle to forgive, and we don't do it often enough, for ourselves or others. The science of forgiveness is fairly straightforward. There is ample clinical research to indicate that forgiveness is a healthy thing for us. Forgiveness has been shown to reduce negative emotional symptoms, to boost immunity, and even improve cardiovascular health.[2] Mechanisms in the brain are pretty simple—we forgive, we feel better. So, this is how I see forgiveness right from the start. Forgiveness is part of the same way we process any negative memory or feeling. Forgiveness is the process of removing the negative feeling associated with a thought. If you say, "I forgive you," but the thought of the transgression still makes you feel resentment, full

---

2. Cohen, "Research on the Science of Forgiveness," para. 18.

forgiveness has not occurred. But we can achieve forgiveness. If we change the way we think, we can change the way we feel.

Commonly, there seems to be distinction made between forgiveness and letting go of resentments. I suppose forgiveness can involve more abstraction than the seeded feelings of resentment. You can "forgive" a politician who publicly apologizes to his constituents for not voting for a bill you wanted more easily than you can let go of resentment toward a friend who failed to support you when you ran for office yourself. The politician's behavior was less personal to you. Resentments, I guess, are more toxic to you—more insidious and festering. But in this dialogue, I am not sure the distinction is that important. This is more a conversation about letting go and getting back. The more you let go, the more you get back.

So, how do we let go or change the way we think? Well, assuming we are talking about small transgressions, such as when your friend eats the last cookie or when your son dents your car, we can usually just let it go via an apology or simply the passage of time. But serious transgressions are far more complicated. Bullying, assault, theft, murder—these are all much more difficult. First and foremost, forgiveness is not the same as not being angry. You can be angry and forgive at the same time; you just can't forgive and have resentments. Second, you may need professional help in working through this. Third, it requires that you try to think about the person, event, or transgression in a different way. Most often, it's about understanding context. Consider a bully as an example. If you step outside your individual personal experience with the bully, you realize he is not just a bully, but also perhaps an athlete, a son, someone who likes pizza and cats. In other words, there is a lot more going on here.

Religious teaching is one way of abstracting the event or person so that the transgression is manageable to us. It is a way of stepping outside of yourself and looking at things differently. It is a way of saying, let me think about this from a different angle. In Anthony's text, God tells us to forgive, and that forgiveness is good. I propose the intention would be to assume that God was in control, and, therefore, we are safe to turn this problem over to Him for Him to manage, in much the same way we as children gave our problems to a parent or elder to manage, or at least try. It doesn't necessarily make the problem go away, but it is reassuring to us to know that someone more capable than ourselves is now in a management position. In that way, if we believe that God will mete out any consequence in a just manner, it is out of our hands, we are no longer in a position of responsibility, and we can move on.

I am not saying that the biblical perspective is wrong. In fact, I am saying it makes sense to me. It fits into my schema where not everything biblical does. But, to me, the ability to forgive rests in putting it outside of how it affects you emotionally and looking at it rationally from another perspective. One option is to look at it from the perspective that we simply can't control the past anyway, and any justice or fairness is a matter of acceptance or understanding. Sometimes, as I said before, that can be accomplished by looking at the transgressors rather than transgressions. Did the person fully intend to hurt you or were you an accidental consequence of the chosen behavior or event? A different kind of abstraction might also apply. How does this event or feeling fit into the larger picture? If you cannot forgive, are you throwing the baby out with the bath water, so to speak? Are you ignoring an entire body of work and just focusing on one mistake? One final question might be: Did this person wake up this morning determined to focus on you and intent on hurting you, or were you somehow an incidental victim?

So, letting go of resentments and forgiving those who have hurt us are closely related. At the end of the day, the question that needs be answered is whether or not anyone benefits from continued anger or holding onto blame. It is my position that hope is optimism, and hope and optimism require a glass-half-full approach. Assuming this, forgiveness is better than the alternative for both the individual and society. Still not convinced? Let's connect the dots.

We have established elsewhere that if you are angry, your brain is focused on protecting you. It circles the wagons and makes sure nothing gets in that can hurt you. While doing this, it has little ability to experience joy. Let's suppose then that you attempted to practice forgiveness. It stands to reason that at least momentarily you would feel better about yourself. This would then potentially release your brain from protective mode by way of endorphin release. The chain reaction would be increased relief, experience of pleasure, and more endorphin release. From there, you transfer your positive feelings to others through a renewed openness and kindness. Using the gratitude loop we discussed elsewhere, you now have begun to improve the world, or at least your little corner of it.

We, in this book, are supposed to be speaking on three different planes, each important in its own way. First, we are discussing the different perspectives of science and religion. Second, we are agreeing to disagree in our discourse with a demonstration of how we can do that respectfully and remain friends. And third, we are showing pathways to hope, disassembling some of those barriers that we or society have built that keep us from positive movement forward. So, number three is the hardest to demonstrate in words. Moving forward starts with a desire to do things differently or a recognition of the destructive effects of blame and lack of forgiveness. It moves then to an understanding that there are real physical benefits to you (and benefits to the greater society) by practicing forgiveness. From there, going back to the beginning, the practice involves changing how you perceive an event and its effects on you.

There is no rule that says what forgiveness must look like. You do not have to like someone more, return to old patterns of relating, or apologize for being angry in order to accomplish forgiveness. You only need to change your mental approach to the event so that it no longer creates a destructive response inside you. The false narrative that we tell ourselves most often is that somehow, we occupy a larger than realistic place in the hurt scenario. For example, we cannot forgive our spouse for lying to us. It's painful, of course, but our false narrative is that the lie was designed to hurt us. In fact, usually the lie was designed to protect the liar. Our spouse lied to avoid consequences, not to hurt us. Looking at it in that way, it is a little easier to feel sympathy, empathy, or pity for the liar. My father died of cancer due to a lifetime of smoking. He pretended to quit smoking several times, effectively lying to his family. When he became ill, it was easy to be angry with him for the years of deceit. However, he wasn't deceiving us to hurt us; he was deceiving us because he was unable to face his perceived inability to stop smoking. We were not the center of the narrative; he was. It wasn't about me; it was about him. It's easier to forgive in that scenario. Compassion is a really good tool in this process, something that seems hard to come by these days.

Anthony

Eric makes some strong points above including this one: *"If we change the way we think, we can change the way we feel."* That hit home with me, and immediately I thought of what the apostle Paul describes in Romans 12 verse 2 (NLT): *"Don't copy the behavior and customs of this world, but let God transform you into a new person by changing the way you think. Then you will learn to know God's will for you, which is good and pleasing and perfect."*

We often become a product of our own thoughts. To take this one step further, our actions are usually born out of our thoughts. Yes, you could say the battlefield is in the mind.

What Paul is referring to when he writes "the world" is the worldly system of resentments, power, materialism, vengeance, jealousy, and the list continues. Paul goes on to write, *"but let God transform you into a new person by changing the way you think."* There it is . . . The NKJV reads, *"The renewing of your mind"*—different words with the same meaning as are all biblical translations.

When we say God transforms hearts, the transformation does not happen by some magical, wishful thinking, or scientific formula. The transformation happens when we apply His principles to our lives. The change happens when we allow hope to take root in our heart, and we have the assurance that His word is true. The transformation happens when we begin trusting in God and truly surrendering our will to His will.

This is not to say that any of us has arrived. We are all works in progress. As we learn more about His ways and truly know Him, as opposed to simply knowing about Him, the difficult things (such as forgiveness) become possible. We begin to know God's will for us which are, in fact, good and pleasing and perfect.

I also think that Eric is on message when he writes of the issue of intent. I believe that in most situations where conflict occurs, the one who initiates the pain didn't set out that day to hurt the other person. You may have heard the saying "hurt people, hurt people," which is commonly referenced on the walls of substance use and mental health centers. The reason is quite simple. There are a lot of hurting people who are attempting to come to terms with or make sense of the hurt that they caused and or the pain others inflicted on them. When you add emotional pain with substance use, it makes for a lot of emotional sorrow, regrets, and shame.

The apostle Paul writes in Colossians 3:13 (NLT), *"Make allowance for each other's faults, and forgive anyone who offends you. Remember, the Lord forgave you, so you must forgive others."*

Considering allowance for others' faults—defensive driving comes to mind. Perhaps you, too, are a defensive driver. First and foremost—thank you! Secondly, what does defensive driving encompass? Defensive drivers anticipate another car cutting them off or running the red light. If we are taking the verses on forgiveness to heart by making allowance for others' faults, forgiveness can become a reality. This is not simply a religious rule. Keeping it is a far deeper concept than that. Forgiveness can truly change your life.

Perhaps it's because God in is infinite wisdom knows the damage of not forgiving. We are operating out of alignment to God's will when we choose not to forgive. It may feel good initially to not forgive someone, but as time goes on, the seed of bitterness begins to grow in our hearts. Often that seed becomes a spiritual poison; it then begins to have major unwanted side effects in our lives. Forgiveness is by no means easy, but it is definitely worth it.

Finding Hope in Hopelessness

Eric

I have to bring this all back to science and hope. We agree that it's in our best interest to forgive, but science proves it. How we do it is up to us, but we benefit from it. Anthony and I both agree that with our current reality being what it is, in politics, climate, economy, and social isolation, we are going to have to let go of some difficult experiences in order to fully embrace new ones, and forgiveness is a part of that.

Chapter 6

Depression

Anthony

I'M GOING TO FOCUS on major depression and how it can be an extremely dark and lonely place. Many of you may have heard this inevitable question, "What do you feel like?" Yes, depression is a place that many do not understand and often don't do much to understand. The initial heartfelt and genuine concern usually fades away with time and is replaced with an underlying anger, shame, and, at times, utter disgust directed at those suffering from depression. Maybe this response is because those who are sincerely trying to provide help simply get very frustrated in the ongoing process. What may seem like words of encouragement from family members and close friends can feel like a flood of demoralizing statements that pour out like an open faucet. Here are a few: "You don't even want to get better." "You like the attention!" "Where is your faith?"

Often each discouraging comment adds another level of resentment to the recipient's already overflowing laundry list of resentments. Yes, an increased level of despair and alienation is added with the feeling of being abandoned by those who you were convinced had your back. For people who are suffering with major depression, it's as if the clock is always ticking on the patience of those around them. It's a continuous and unstable walk on eggshells from the one with depression and those trying to find a solution.

Let's explore the infamous remark, "Where's your faith?" Yes, now even the individual's faith is up for debate. While a person is suffering from depression, nothing is off limits during pursuit of assigning blame for this difficult and seemingly endless situation. As you may know, faith is a sensitive and at times an explosive topic, so much so that wars have been fought over it throughout the years. (I'm at a loss to understand where the teaching of Christ to love one another fits in with that, but that's for another book.)

When providing encouragement to those who are in emotional despair and in great need of some hope, do not question their faith. Only God knows our hearts, and you may later be surprised to learn that it was faith that kept them afloat.

I'm writing this from my own experience on this subject and on other subjects being discussed in this book. It may seem harsh, but it is all too often reality. I am now blessed with the incredible opportunity to try to encourage and provide faith counsel at this amazing company called Banyan Treatment Centers. *"And we know that in all things God works for the good of those who love him, who] have been called according to his purpose."* Romans 8:28 (NIV)

There is hope in any situation, no matter how difficult because God doesn't waste any suffering. It is not about our purpose but His purpose. This may not be easy to understand during the storms of life, but it will make sense at some point. We live our lives looking forward, and we understand it looking backwards. Allow Him to turn a mess into a message.

So, if you are someone who has dealt with this hideous thing called depression for your entire life or it made its appearance through some traumatic situation as in my case, know that there is hope in hopelessness! God is in the restoration business and can pull you out of the pit of despair. I have not had depression since April of 2013. Now, the question I am most frequently asked when speaking on this topic is in complete contrast to the demoralizing questions listed above. The question now is one I love to answer rather than cower from. This beautiful question from so many people suffering is this: "How did you get past the depression?"

It's a sincere question that those who are in this dark maze are truly and genuinely waiting to hear the answer. I love the question because many times after answering it, there is a glimmer of hope in the person's sad eyes, and it gives me the opportunity to share the truth of not *what* set me free from absolute misery but *Who* set me free. I think one of the best ways to describe it in a concise manner is Psalm 34:6 (NKJV) *"This poor man cried out, and the Lord heard him, and saved him out of all his troubles."*

After years of blaming God and others for all my suffering, I actually cried out to Him holding nothing back. This may come across to some as an overly simplistic pipe dream, but it's true. There are also eighty-five verses throughout the Bible that tell us when we seek God with *all* our heart, we will find Him. That makes all the difference. I was no longer simply using God when I needed something, but I had begun a relationship with Him.

These are no longer simply words in an ancient book; they now jump off the page at me. I lived it out and I know the words are true. These verses can play out and become truth in your own life with your own suffering and struggles. As the saying goes, my only regret was that I didn't do it sooner. Maybe you haven't taken God up on this offer to truly find Him, but the amazing thing is, with God, His offer still stands.

Eric

Anthony speaks so profoundly of faith. Faith, as it would end up, was and remains the catalyst for change in his life. So, what is faith? At least in part, I think many would agree with the following: Faith is the suspension of need to "know," in response to the desire to "believe." Faith gives us the ability to "believe" in possibility. In turn, possibility allows us the opportunity to *hope*. Hope is a major key in the battle that so many people face with depression. Depression makes hope seem more and more remote. But recovery is possible, and hope can and will return. Recovery from depression requires the suspending of the need to feel better right this very minute and replacing it with hope that soon you will feel a little better, one minute or day at a time.

Depression is not a feeling. Depression is not a thing. Depression is not an event. Depression is a plethora of experiences and concepts. It's a cluster of symptoms and situations. Clinically speaking, it is a pervasive experience of ongoing feeling for months or years of what we consider negative emotion. Depression is not always experienced as sadness. It could also be anger, restlessness, anxious or overwhelming feelings or just omnipresent feelings of hopelessness, helplessness, and decreased self-worth, difficulty concentrating, or insomnia.[1] *The American Psychiatric Association: Diagnostic and Statistical Manual of Mental Disorders*, (DSM–5), lists 8 kinds of depression.[2] Some types of depression can be debilitating, causing one to want to lie in bed or deny oneself care or to contemplate suicide. Some types I have seen cause excessive energy, inability to sleep, and even psychosis. But all depression has some common elements—difficulty in seeing a way out, before loneliness, isolation, and hopelessness result.

Anthony spoke of shame. He described it as put upon him by others, as they questioned how he could allow himself to be in his condition. Shame is the embarrassment at a profound level of your state. Who wants to share that with others? How can you not feel lonely or even completely alone? Many of us with depression can describe feeling alone in a group of people, in a conversation, or at a party. An inability to connect to the world and the resulting feelings of being somehow broken—it's familiar to us.

I, too, have dealt with depression. My family has a history of it. Many families do.[3] I grew up feeling sad, cynical, and angry. It wasn't like I wore it on my sleeve; most people would not have guessed. But I was sad. I was prone to isolation. I hurt people. I was insecure and ashamed at times. Some days, weeks, years were

1. Rabins and Gallo, "Depression without Sadness," 820–826.

2. American Psychiatric Association(DSM–5), 155.

3. Van Dijk, et al, "Association of Multigenerational,"778.

better than others, but I so often felt like I wanted to feel better. As it is commonly described in popular culture, I wore a disguise of someone who was happy and in control. Yet, I never felt quite right. I often used humor to deflect how I was feeling inside, as I am guessing many people do. I was great at parties—funny and energetic and willing to go all night. But inside, I was alone with myself, and sometimes it felt grim and desolate. Did I abuse substances to feel better? You bet I did. Did it work? Sure. Sometimes. For a while. Not really.

In my early 20's I was studying for my master of social work degree, so I was connected to a whole bunch of helpful people. Several times a week, after classes, we would head to the local pub to process what we were learning and to unwind. Over time, I began to confide in my comrades more and more about what was going on behind the veneer. I told them the truth—that I felt sad all the time, as if there was a hole in my soul. My friends told me the obvious: to seek therapy! So, I did, and I do to this day from time to time. As the result of this first experience, I accepted a trial of antidepressant medications. I soon found them to give me the ability to level things out emotionally. After being on them for a few months, I recognized that I had not felt the "hole in my soul" for some time. I realized that this was perhaps how other people felt—how "normal people" felt. It gave me hope and confidence. I had a new belief that things could be different. Interesting to some might be that it was at that time, that the first professional in my life told me that maybe alcohol was affecting my happiness as well. I did not take that to heart, but more on that later.

Today, age has given to wisdom (at least a little), and I look at things differently. Sadness is necessary for the experience and value of joy. Sadness gives rise to creativity. Sadness can connect us. We love to feel sad at a movie or when listening to a song, or even when retelling the Easter story, as it connects us to others in a compassionate way and gives us hope for redemption and release. I don't take medications now; I have developed my own understanding (or faith) that I am okay, regardless of my emotions. I have developed a better understanding of my feelings, of what they mean, and how to cope.

I have learned to tell on myself. It is a powerful thing to tell another person that you don't feel well. When I do, I am not asking people to feel sorry for me, just to understand that I am struggling a little today, this week, this year. I learned that depression, like so many of the things we talk about in this book, is related to brain chemistry. It has to do with dopamine and serotonin. It's not something I can snap out of or get over quickly. It is something that I have to manage, like my diet or my work. I think about it every day and decide what is best for me to do to maximize my productivity. Sometimes I am righter than others. Therapists have helped me get here. Maybe God put therapists in the world to help people like me. Maybe there are more random reasons why I feel better today than I used to, but somehow, I doubt it. Be it from science or God, hope has to come from somewhere.

Anthony

I often find this to be true while researching clinical perspectives on various topics—the verses and clinical studies or secular viewpoints are quite similar. Such is the case here. Eric's eloquent description of faith is very similar to one book in the Bible, Hebrews, which is very faith focused. Consider Hebrews 11:1 (NKJ) "*Now faith is the substance of things hoped for, the evidence of things not seen.*" Different words from different points of view, yet we once again arrive at the same place. This is, by no means, an isolated incident. So many times, when referencing the major players in the healthcare industry, such as the Mayo Clinic or other secular studies conducted by towering intellects, we see that they, without knowing it, are saying very similar things that are in God's Word.

I am in agreement with Eric's assessment of the D word, and I applaud his transparency on the subject. I think he hit the nail on the head with this profound statement: "*. . . difficulty in seeing a way out.*" I often make attempts to describe what I was feeling when suffering with depression as being in an emotional maze with no way out. I also think the following is quite profound regarding shame: *"Shame is the embarrassment at a profound level of your state. Who wants to share that with others?"*

We often keep things we are embarrassed about or ashamed of very close to the vest. This, as well, would have to apply to depression in many cases. The shame that's attached to depression is sometimes more destructive than the depression itself.

In reality, I believe most people want to share what's going on in their head and heart, but when becoming vulnerable, we are sometimes met with judgment which will lead the depressed person right back to shutting down and concealing their true suffering and emotional pain. The late Robin Williams may have said it best, *"People don't fake depression . . . they fake being okay."*[4] This is from a man who made millions of people laugh, and he's no longer with us. Perhaps he would still be here making the world forget about their own pain if he had been truly able to be open about his own pain.

At about 11:45 a.m. on Aug. 11, 2014, Williams' assistant grew concerned. He slipped a note under the door, and then picked the lock. He found the comedian dressed in a long black T-shirt and belted black jeans, and hanging by a nylon belt in a closet door frame. The actor, who was being treated for severe depression, also had cuts on his wrist.[5]

We agree. People, like Robin Williams or you or me, strive to be well, not sick. Those who do not are merely manifesting their illness, not their desire or destiny. Condemnation and shame are hurtful. Providing hope, however, can be the light out of the darkness.

Eric

I could not complete this dialogue without reinforcing the last points made about suicide. Suicide is likely the most painful and difficult potential outcome of depression. Suicide is rampant in

---

4. Svoboda, "Quotes of Famous People," n.p.

5. Youn, "Robin Williams: Autopsy Confirms," para. 5.

our society, and I have seen it in my work far more than I ever dreamed possible. Suicide is absolutely preventable, and there are always alternatives to taking your own life. This discussion in these pages cannot begin to capture the complexities of this issue, so I will simply say that people do care, there is always hope. If you or anyone you know is thinking about suicide, please call the national suicide prevention lifeline at 800–273-8255.

In my experience as a clinician, I have seen many different versions of unhappy people. I have also read countless research articles that break down what depression is, how it affects and is affected by the brain, and what can be done about it. Although it does happen from time to time, most people do not seek therapy just to bounce a few good ideas around or to discuss how happiness is causing problems in life. Most often, people have been sad, angry, sleepless, distracted, or otherwise emotionally struggling, and often exhibiting signs of depression. The good news is, that as mental health problems go, these can be some of the simpler ones to address. There are numerous scientifically proven approaches that make a difference. I have helped countless people find some relief through therapeutic intervention. I have worked with folks who have been too depressed to speak or get out of bed, and I have worked with people who just can't shake feeling blue, and I have seen both find relief in therapy.

In my own life, I have been prescribed and have found relief in medication, made dietary changes, found a regimen of exercise that worked for me, and perhaps, most effective in my understanding of my own depressed symptoms, I have learned the practice of acceptance. I believe all of these steps and changes made a real difference in how my brain processed information and dramatically impacted my outlook.

Anthony

Eric made some excellent points on the topic of suicide, and, tragically with this being so pervasive these days, suicide is an extremely concerning matter. As Eric clearly pointed out above,

"Suicide is likely the most painful and difficult potential outcome of depression."

As a Chaplain, I have performed numerous memorial services. I have also been asked the questions many times by family members, "What happens to someone who commits suicide?" It's not the most comfortable question to field, but many are genuinely and sometimes desperately seeking an answer. My answer comes from what the Bible says on the subject. There were seven people who committed suicide in the Bible. You are probably familiar with the suicide of Judas Iscariot who took his own life after betraying Jesus.

We have insight as to the circumstances surrounding the act of suicide, but the Bible is silent on the eternal destination of those who commit suicide. There has been intense debate on both sides of the question from scholars and people with no faith affiliation. I believe God didn't say either way because if people believed they were going to Heaven, there would be many more people taking their own lives. If it was written that they were going to hell, the pain may be more than the loved one could bear. Suicide is tragic and is another sobering issue that clearly points to the tremendous suffering in the world.

I want to close with this true story. A neighbor shared with me that his close friend's son at twenty-seven years old hanged himself. His mother was the first to find him two days later. First responders said judging from the scene his pit-bull terrier never left his side. I noticed for the first time in over two years while sharing this heartbreaking story, my neighbor began petting my pit-bull terrier, Luke. My neighbor kept repeating with tears in his eyes, "These dogs are loyal." The story really hit home for me on two levels—the horrible human suffering and the loyalty and unconditional love of his dog. It hit me hard because there was a period of time in my life when I, too, was completely hopeless and broken in spirit. I truly believed this world would be better without me in it. But God showed up with His amazing love, mercy, peace, and restoring power. He also blessed me with my beloved dog Luke. There are a lot of hurting people out there who are in desperate need of hope and some compassion. Check in with your neighbors, share some encouraging words to someone who you think needs it, and pray for them. You never know the impact it may have on someone; it may even save a life.

Chapter 7

Anger

Anthony

WHAT HAS ANGER COST you in your life? Maybe it's a relationship, friends, family members, your freedom, or perhaps just the allusive peace of mind. In this chapter we are going to discuss the topic of anger. From a faith perspective there is another type of anger which you may not be as familiar with that is called righteous anger or righteous indignation.

You may have heard the story of when Jesus became angry and began turning over the tables in the temple courtyard. This was in response, and a result of, people defiling the temple. In fact, Jesus actually did it twice nearly three years apart. The first time was just after His first miracle of turning water into wine at the wedding in Cana. It can be found in John 2:7–16 (NKJ).

The second cleansing of the temple came when Jesus was entering Jerusalem on the last week of His life, a time that is often referenced as the Passion week.

This is recorded in Matthew, Mark, and Luke. Let's consider Matthew 21:13 (NLT).

Jesus said to them, "The Scriptures declare, '*My Temple will be called a house of prayer, but you have turned it into a den of thieves!*'" Let's break this down as it relates to what Jesus demonstrated which was righteous anger or "righteous indignation" as a result of sin taking place in front of the temple.

Let's relate righteous anger to current times. Say you are walking into your church, and as you walk in, there are people selling drugs. Would you experience anger? Another illustration that I experience all too often is when I witness animals being abused or abandoned. This may be difficult to believe, but the abandonment increases right before Christmas as people who have no business ever owning a pet simply leave their older dogs somewhere to make room for a Christmas puppy. Some Christmas present for the poor dogs who now find themselves alone in a shelter or far worse! Yes, this infuriates me, but it also motivates me to do something about it. Perhaps it's some other cause that is close to your heart. So, righteous anger could manifest itself into a great cause that impacts many people, such as the cause of MADD—Mothers Against Drunk Driving.

Mothers Against Drunk Driving, a nonprofit organization, was founded in 1980 by Candace Lightner, a mother whose daughter was killed by an impaired motorist in California. MADD aims "to end drunk driving, help fight drugged driving, support victims of these violent crimes, and prevent underage drinking."[1] of these violent crimes, and prevent underage drinking."[1]

Another foundation which had its origins in tragedy and tremendous anger is the America's Missing: Broadcast Emergency Response. Yes, the AMBER Alert. This was the result of the horrible loss of life in Arlington, Texas, back in 1996. The system is named for Amber Rene Hagerman, the victim of an unsolved child murder case. As of December 31,2021, 1,111 children were rescued specifically because of AMBER Alert![2]

Let's move on to the anger that you may be all too familiar with that creates pain and chaos in our lives and in the lives of those around us. The anger is often intertwined with thoughts or

1. Mothers Against Drunk Driving (MADD), homepage.
2. "About Amber Alert," see history/statistics.

ways to get even. These considerations of retaliation will vary from simply no longer speaking with someone or in other cases, such as retaliations, can escalate to a far more dangerous place. The apostle Paul writes in Ephesians 4:26, *"In your anger do not sin: Do not let the sun go down while you are still angry."*

I believe the two main takeaways are these: First, there are going to be times when we are going to get angry no matter how hard we try not to; anger is a natural emotion. The second may be one of those golden nuggets of wisdom your parents or grandparents told you, like "Don't go to bed angry." I know I heard that before, but actually applying it was a totally different story. Hopefully this will make some sense. Another illustration may be in order here. Trying to completely eliminate anger is similar to trying to lose weight by saying you are not going to eat anymore. Take it from me; I have employed that weight-loss strategy. It doesn't work! A better approach is to consider managing the upset. Think of it like managing the cold weather in the northern parts of the country in the winter. You may wear a coat, gloves, and hat. I hate to disappoint my global warming friends, but it will inevitably get cold there. Let's look at some ways to manage the anger. I'm pulling from my own experience with anger before I became a Christian, of course . . . wink.

Back in 2014, I was a part of a ministry where I would facilitate Bible studies at the South Florida Reception Center in Doral, Florida. Reception center might sound like a nice tranquil place to visit; however, it was anything but tranquil. It was a very rough Florida State prison where inmates were recently sentenced and were often extremely angry. Any hope of release through the court system had come to a grinding halt. I would meet with fifty or sixty inmates who had, you guessed it, *major* anger issues. I titled my study "Biblical Anger Resolution." The cold and cramped room was filled. To be completely honest, the capacity crowd in attendance wasn't due to my incredible teaching. The inmates actually didn't have much choice.

One inmate always seemed very engaged. He came up to me after one of the meetings and told me that when he first came into the prison, he was filled with hatred and anger toward his girlfriend. Apparently, he had written to her a very horrible, hate-filled, and threatening letter. He said the letter happened to get returned to him a few months later. At this point he had a much better handle on his anger issues. He read the letter and said he could not believe what he had written. He said he tore up two of the three pages and revised the third.

He realized that in his state of rage, he wrote things which he regretted and would have caused even more suffering for his girlfriend and himself.

He smiled as he was sharing this, as if to say that he finally did the right thing. While speaking with this man, I realized the importance of not responding in the state of anger. This man who was incarcerated for what, I didn't ask, but I know was not a good thing, taught me a valuable life lesson. If we allow ourselves time to calm down, think things through, and look at it from the other person's perspective, we have a much better shot at avoiding conflicts in life. The other lesson was, if we actually listen to someone, regardless of what status society brands them with or someone we may not even see eye to eye with, it's still possible that the person can teach us valuable life lessons. I saw hope in his eyes and a genuine sense of accomplishment. Although he probably didn't realize it, the man encouraged me while I was there trying to encourage him. I believe if we replace the judgment with a listening ear, we can learn something and be encouraged in the most unlikely of places. This also applies with substance abuse and mental health centers. I am here to try to provide some hope and encouragement, but many times, I am the one who is encouraged!

Eric

Anger is an interesting emotion for me. I find that many people, in the simplest of terms, do not grasp that anger encompasses a wide range of experiences. Many people equate anger with rage and violence. While rage and violence generally rely on anger for their existence, so do less recognizable forms or variants, such as bitterness, resentment, distrust, sarcasm, and cynicism. Anthony clearly references biblical experiences of rage, great injustice, resentment, and vengeance. For many of us, it's not about that. For many of us, it's just about this low-level feeling of frustration or stress that seems to eat at us. It just pervades our perception by making us see everything through a negative lens, keeping us from experiencing peace or joy.

Anger is a basic emotion. In healthy individuals, it exists as an original piece to the classic fight or flight response. When an individual is threatened or perceives a threat, the survival hormones, primarily adrenaline and cortisol, are activated. This results in a hyper-defensive state that causes us, theoretically, to defend ourselves. We can do that by assertively speaking or aggressively acting. Once the threat is over, we return to a normal state of increased relaxation.[3]

Since most of us in our daily lives do not often have true life-threatening experiences, anger is activated in other ways. It is activated through feelings of being wronged, by perceived injustices, by embarrassment or humiliation, or by other "threats" to our sense of self. Each of us also has a different hormonal make up. Some of us have higher levels of testosterone, for example, than others. These individuals have a higher propensity to experience higher levels of anger.

Anger is also activated by our own ongoing defenses when we view the world as hostile toward us. As individuals develop and grow from birth to adulthood, they develop schema or "tape recordings" about how the world works and how they belong in it. These "tapes" are incorporated into our sense of "self." When we build a conceptual framework that everyone is judging us, no one likes us, we are not as good as other people, or that if we trust someone, they will hurt us, we experience anger. Unfortunately, this is not anger that goes away, because the threat is perceived as being part of our experiences. The "tapes," that we must protect ourselves from harm, play all day long in our heads. So, we react. We lash out at others. We are irritable. We push people away. We

3. "Anger, Hostility, and Violent Behavior," sec. 1.

use sarcasm or put downs and hurt other people before they can hurt us. We express cynical or pessimistic views of the world. We protect ourselves by isolation, avoidance, and lashing out, which in turn can raise our levels of loneliness or even depression.

Rage is something I have never really experienced. Rage is the extreme emotional release of anger, where violent acting out is the primary symptom. I am not built for rage, I would guess. My hormonal balances of one or the other never seem to tip the scale in this direction. Those who are inclined toward rage have often experienced a great deal of success by attending anger management courses. Science says they work well for many.[4]

I like to think about anger for myself in a couple different ways. First, if I have become angry once, say, in one day, then it is very possible that someone or something else on the outside of my body has caused me to become angry. In that case, I attempt to resolve the anger by one of my coping skills, usually talking about it or by weighing its value vs. the rest of the things I have on my mind. (If prayer works for you, then by all means, pray). If I have become angry twice in a day, or if my anger lasts for longer than an hour or so, then it is probably something on the inside.[5] It is probably me.

When this happens, I need to do two things. First, I need to run a body check. Did I sleep well last night? Am I hungry? Have I had a lot of sad or angry thoughts recently? Or am I carrying a resentment or frustration that I need to talk about? Second, I need to tell on myself. I need to talk about it. I tell someone that I am feeling angry, and that I am not sure why, and that I am sorry if I am aloof, overly sarcastic, short, or even mean. Then I ask for support and patience. Often, this self-check and appropriate intervention of eating, resting, or seeking support will diffuse my feelings.

As I talked about earlier and will mention as we move forward, our "tapes" are always playing in our heads. We have the power to change those tapes over time, into tapes that say happier, kinder,

4. Castella, "Luis Suarez: Does Anger Management Actually Work?" para. 18.

5. Kahn, "What's Causing My Agitation?" sec. 1.

more trustful things perhaps. Cognitive Behavioral Therapy, the therapy framework behind most anger management classes and other successful interventions, is extremely useful in helping us challenge our beliefs of how the world works and how we should react to it.[6]

I think maybe it's a modern notion that anger is bad, perhaps because we have so few true threats to our safety in comparison to our more aggressive elders. But it's okay to get angry. Everybody does, and everybody should. It's okay to get angry over sex, money, injustice, or aggression toward you. It is simply self-destructive to not do what is necessary to process the emotion, to work through it, and to strive to not allow it to be harmful beyond its purpose. I am strongly opined that logic and calm during anger give us roads to resolution, and we can master more than we thought possible.

So, let's just make sure this is understood. Anger is an emotion. Violence is only one possible outcome of anger. Violence, including yelling, threatening someone, throwing things or physically hitting someone and a host of other like behaviors, is just that—a set of behaviors. In my life, I make it a strong point to choose non-violent expression of anger. No one is going to listen to me if I am threatening them or screaming at them. They will be too busy trying to defend themselves emotionally or physically. It is only when I express my anger constructively that the situation gets resolved positively. Anger is not bad. It exists to protect you. If it is hurting you, get help. You can learn to experience anger differently.

For those who don't see hope here, it is found by looking at it this way: Anger is good. It motivates and protects us. Rage is destructive, but it doesn't have to control us. Anger helps us experience opposite or contrasting emotion, so it allows us to know calm and joy in ways otherwise not possible. What's not hopeful about that?

---

6. Pagán, "Cognitive Behavioral Therapy (CBT)," sec. 1, 2.

Anthony

This chapter can very well be another perfect example of why Eric and I wanted to collaborate on this book. Eric's anger, as he explains above, is quite the contrast from the anger that I experienced for much of my life prior to deepening my relationship with God and applying His principles to my life. I am by no means perfect, but I am now a far cry from how I used to operate during that time when my previous life was in the investigations and corporate security industry. Maybe my anger at that time stemmed from the environment and the aggressive culture or maybe my anger was fed by the wrongly perceived notion that aggression was a sign of strength in an environment where kindness was perceived as weakness.

Whatever the origins, my take on anger from personal experience and witnessing it on an almost a daily basis in those days brings me to the conclusion that anger is more pervasive than many would think. In retrospect, I am grateful that Eric is not the full of rage and aggressive type since my office is across the hall from his and he oversees every aspect of the company. (This was probably my failed attempt to inject humor into the potentially destructive and serious topic of anger.)

I think the reason I look at anger from a different perspective now is because, by God's grace, I am in the process of experiencing the life-changing heart transformation that I know could happen only through the power of Christ. I am also blessed to have a front row seat at Banyan's Faith in Recovery program over the past six plus years and have witnessed the same kind of metamorphosis in countless people who have been in our program. The change is, by no means, a result of behavior modification but something far deeper, far more profound. No, the change is the result of a genuine transformation of the heart! God loves us just the way we are, but He loves us too much to allow us to stay that way. If you are looking for evidence of God, look for people who unsuccessfully made every effort to change on their own *will* and finally were able to change through His *power*.

Chapter 8

Fear

Anthony

THERE ARE THREE HUNDRED sixty-five verses in the Bible that direct us not to fear. Could this just be another coincidence or is God in the middle of it? In our Faith in Recovery program at Banyan Treatment Centers, we call these things God-incidences, so with three hundred sixty-five days in a year (one verse for each day), maybe God is trying to tell us that He doesn't want us to live in fear! This kind of fear is not a sense of nervousness that most of us experience before a major presentation. It's not a sudden dread of having to tell your mom you've broken her favorite vase. (That was a Brady Bunch episode reference for all you Baby Boomers out there.) Let's get back to the topic at hand. Here we are focusing on a level of fear that consumes people and limits them from reaching their full potential. The phrase "I was scared stiff" may come to mind or "paralyzed by fear." For some, being paralyzed by fear is not too far from their reality.

How about "paralysis by analysis"—when we analyze something so much that we never make a decision, but what happens is, time makes the decision for us, and we may not like the outcome.

Second guessing, for not making the decision when we had the opportunity to do so, takes center stage. I have been there, that's for sure! Fear limits us from our true potential and the purposes God has for our lives. We can only really go to the point where fear allows us to go. In a sense, fear puts up a roadblock for our hopes and dreams. In many cases fear simply sends us down a dead-end road. Fear can also open the door to the regret in our lives. So many people have the God-given ability to do something, but let fear stop them in their tracks!

Let's look at a definition of fear: "A distressing emotion aroused by impending danger, evil, pain, etc., whether the threat is real or imagined; the feeling or condition of being afraid."[1] I believe the key words in this definition are "whether the threat is real or imagined." How many times have you feared the outcome of an impending bad situation, but that outcome never happened? What *did* happen was a waste of a lot of energy, time, and a great loss of peace of mind.

Second Timothy 1:7 (NKJ) reads, *"For God has not given us a spirit of fear, but of power and of love and of a sound mind."* In this passage Paul is contrasting fear with love, power, and a sound mind. That's a hefty price to pay for something that may or may not even happen.

How about this verse from 1 John 4:18 (ESV)? *"There is no fear in love, but perfect love casts out fear. For fear has to do with punishment, and whoever fears has not been perfected in love."*

So, whether you are a person of faith or not, the fact remains that in many cases we pay a price for our fears. If you are a person who truly believes that Scripture is the inspired word of God, my question to you is simply this: Why are you still living in fear?

Eric

Fear is an emotion. It is a heightened state of awareness that tells us that there is a threat to us. It can be the result, as Anthony states, of

1. "Fear."

a real or perceived event or circumstance. While not all of us have experienced all emotions in the extreme, at one point or another, all of us have been fearful and even terrified. Fear is an emotion. It is a state of arousal that says to our body we have to make quick choices about what to do next. Do we fight or run, or scream, cower or freeze? We do these things in a moment, until the danger passes, and the fear subsides.

Living in fear is an entirely different thing. The implication here is that we exist day-to-day looking over our shoulders as to what threat is next, or worse, that the same threat does not subside, and, therefore, we cannot let our guard down. Living in fear is a reference to chronicity. This manifests itself in many common, and in some not so common, experiences.

Stress is how some people might experience this. We are all familiar with how stress feels to some degree. In this world, it comes with feelings of being overwhelmed, not being able to keep up, or juggling too many balls in the air. Stress can feel like a weight on your shoulders or like a drain on your brain. It is tied to weight gain and loss, difficulty in concentrating, changes in blood pressure, difficulty with sleep, and increased anxiety, agitation, and depression.[2] Stress is a health crisis in the United States with more people feeling stressed than ever.[3]

Anxiety is similar to stress but involves more acute feelings of fear and has a more direct connection to your thoughts of impending trouble or even doom. Anxiety has so many implications for our health and is such a huge problem for many of us. We will discuss this later.

Phobia is a type of anxiety that relates to unfounded or embellished fear of something that poses a perceived threat that far outweighs actual threat. This is specific in nature, meaning that it tends to focus on specific things, but it can be extremely debilitating. Sometimes phobias are based on past experiences. Sometimes the origin of the phobia is less clear. Phobias about interacting with others, or leaving the house, or about fearing heights, bridges or

---

2. "Stress and Your Health," sec. 1–3.

3. Mastroianni, "More Stressed than Ever," sec. 1–3.

certain animals or insects are common, but can keep people prisoners in their own homes.[4] Social phobia is a hot topic in recent years and phobias about illness are, of course, particularly relevant in our current world of pandemic infections. Unfortunately, I believe they are worsened by divisive and shaming behaviors in the media and politics.

Paranoia is a term generally attached to a fear that is not based on reality at all. This is a fear that you, perhaps, are being watched or followed, or that someone is out to do you harm, when there is no real evidence to support the fear. In popular culture, paranoia can be a way to describe insecurity and anxiety. For example, one might say that he or she was "paranoid that everyone hated me after that party." In clinical terms, paranoia can be used to describe a type of psychosis, related directly to mental illness. This more severe type of paranoia is a suspicious fear and is not likely to subside without help from professionals.[5]

There is significant interest and literature about panic and panic attacks. These acute episodes of fear are increasingly reported as common and have been used to describe a wide range of severe, rapid onset of anxiety and fear, with shortness of breath, rapid heartbeat and other physical symptoms.[6] Many of us have experienced feeling "overly anxious," but a panic attack can be debilitating for sure. Panic attacks are relatively common and can be treated.[7]

So, why do we live in fear, and what do we do about it? The Bible, Anthony says, holds a message of relief for those who trust in God and those who follow His word. Beyond or apart from that, there are myriad interventions that are effective with each of the above issues. Hormonal therapies are controversial but effective for many of the stress and anxiety related issues, especially in women. Antidepressants and neuroleptic medications can assist in some of these issues as well, particularly paranoia and anxiety. Cognitive behavioral and behavioral therapies are proven effective

4. Brazier, "Everything You Need to Know about Phobias," sec. 1–3.
5. Frysh, "Paranoia: Symptoms, Causes, and Treatments," sec. 1–7.
6. "Panic Attacks and Panic Disorders," sec. 1–3.
7. "Panic Disorders," sec. 4.

in managing or alleviating stress, panic, anxiety, and phobia, by teaching the body to react differently to the information it is receiving from its environment.[8] Most of what we experience that might be called "living in fear" is in reaction to incorrect messaging between the environment and the brain. Whether it's a bridge that is safely crossed by thousands of persons per day, or a test that you are prepared for, or the meeting you are about to enter, or the bill that you can't afford to pay, none are likely to cause you physical harm, which is the real purpose of fear. Since most of us are not constantly living in harm's way, it is a matter of teaching the body to believe it is safe with you, and that you can meet most of life's challenges. You've got this.

Each one of these issues is separate and should be diagnosed accurately by a professional if you are going to seek treatment. For general stress and anxiety, many people find self-help ideas useful, like taking walks, exercising, meditating, minding diet, taking warm baths, and other relaxing pursuits.

Other issues raised are issues of trust. Trust is integral in being unafraid. Trust is confidence, trust is belief in something or someone, and trust is allowing yourself the gift of knowing that no matter how much you wish something to be so, you simply cannot control everything. Relinquish some of the notion that you always have to be in control, or that you must not err or fail, and you will move mountains of fear out of your path.

Anthony

Eric draws the clear distinction between the types of fear and the outcomes that result from them. The emotion of fear is something I believe God has wired us with for self-preservation. It's a temporary, situational fear that comes upon us to alert us that impending pain or danger is near. This type of fear could save your life.

The fear that is not from God is the kind of fear that is evidenced by those three hundred sixty-five biblical reference points

8. "Anxiety Disorders," sec. 4.

above where we are told not to live in this specific kind of fear. This kind of fear that consumes us is perpetual as referenced earlier "the spirit of fear," the kind that God warns us against.

I was consumed with this self-limiting fear for seven years. During this agonizing period of time, I tried, time after time, all the conventional approaches to rid myself of this suffering, but none of the standard approaches worked. It was not until I truly began to restore my relationship with God and began to apply His approach to conquering fear did things dramatically change for the better. I have not looked back. I now choose to look only to Him. I no longer focus on the problem, which, often times, is me. I focus on the solution which comes from knowing God.

You may remember hearing of David's Psalm 23 when you were growing up:

"Yea, though I walk through the valley of the shadow of death, I will fear no evil; for You are with me;" Psalm 23:4 (NKJ).

David had many legitimate reasons to be fearful during that time, but he chose not to be afraid because he had faith that God was with him. God didn't remove David's storms of life; what God did was carry David through those difficult times. God does the same thing today.

Most of the time He does not remove our difficult circumstances as quickly as we would like because He's trying to change our hearts as He walks with us through the difficult situations.

So, begin to choose faith over fear, and remember, faith in God includes faith in His timing, and His timing is perfect!

Chapter 9

Grief

Eric

GOOD GRIEF! GRIEF IS something we all experience at one point or another. It is the emotional response to the experience of losing someone or something to which we are emotionally attached. Normally, we think of grief after the death of a loved one. However, grief can be for a lot of things. We can grieve the loss of a relationship, a home, a way of life, health, or anything we lose or have a threat of losing. Okay, so grief is all that and more, but important to us here, is that grief can be hard, really hard, to shake.

Years ago, many of us heard of the five stages of grief, thanks to the groundbreaking work of Elisabeth Kübler-Ross. Dr. Kübler-Ross spent a lifetime studying the impact of death and dying on the individual and the surrounding social network. The concept of grief was broken down into phases we were believed to pass through—from denial, to anger, bargaining, depression, and finally acceptance.[1] This gave both the practitioner and the client a wonderful roadmap to follow. There was only one problem; it really didn't work that way. It really turns out that we all grieve differently,

---

1. Kübler-Ross and Byock, *On Death and Dying*, 34,44,72,75,98.

and no roadmap truly exists.[2] However, the long-term benefits of Dr. Kübler-Ross's work were, in my opinion, twofold. One is that there still exists that concept that grief can take on different faces, if not different stages per se. The other is that Dr. Kübler-Ross opened the door to speak about death and dying in ways I was not comfortable with before, by demystifying the process that is so natural.

But grief isn't necessarily about death, is it? It's about a whole host of losses, and even just changes, really. And grief in adversity is not about typical grief either. Truth is, most of us lose a loved one, or a pet, or a friend at some point. Most of us feel heartache, emotional pain, and sadness. Many of us cry, feel really bad for a days or weeks, and eventually start to feel better over time. But sometimes, grief happens when we least expect it, and lingers far longer than we expect, and we start to feel broken. Sometimes a breakup with a girl or boyfriend, a loss of a job, retirement, sale of a home or move, or life change like sobriety or even the loss of perceived youth could make you grieve over what you had.

I remember twenty years ago, when I was leaving Michigan to move to Florida. The change was exciting for me and my family, and I looked forward to it greatly, as a new start, or a new chapter. The problem was that I did not anticipate that this also meant the end of the old start, or the old chapter. I remember saying goodbye to my best friend and driving away from my empty house on my way to the highway. It hit me suddenly that I would never have the same relationships with those people or that house or that life again, and I broke down. I had a physical reaction that made me pull over for fear of a driving disaster. It's not like I hadn't thought about it; I just hadn't really felt it until then.

I have plenty of examples, perhaps too personal, for these pages, but the idea is the same. We all know these pains. I know friends who can't "let go" of their past, and I believe it's grief that sticks them. But I am not sure that many of us discuss that lingering grief all of the time because we might not recognize it as such. Grief sometimes looks like crying, sadness, and withdrawal. But sometimes it looks different. You might wonder, "What's wrong

2. McVean, "It's Time to Let the Five Stages of Grief Die," para. 6.

with me? Why don't I feel sad?" Well, it could be that grief is just different this time. Maybe this time you have lost your appetite, you find yourself avoiding situations that remind you of your loss, or perhaps you can't sleep. Perhaps you are quick to anger, or are unmotivated to complete something you start, when you used to be a go-getter.[3] Maybe you can't concentrate lately at work. Maybe, your grief just looks different.

Technically, there are several different types of grief which are frequently referenced.[4] Common types are anticipatory grief, complicated grief, and sudden grief. Anticipatory grief is that feeling associated with getting ready to say goodbye during a long illness or a planned departure. Complicated grief is that which does not go away but lingers. Lingering grief feeds off itself, I think, and it seems like one would have to feel a little abnormal, asking, "Why can't I get over this?" For me, anticipatory grief has also been something problematic. Several of my family members have passed away after long illnesses. While loving them profoundly, I found that the long anticipation of the loss became a lot to manage, and it inevitably left me with feelings that were ambiguous at best. I know that I am not alone when I say that at times, I just wished that my loved one would finally pass, so that they and I could find peace. I had been grieving so long, I felt like I was "ready." That is not a comfortable feeling to have, but I think it happens more than we want to admit.

So, therapy can really help with grief. It's a common topic in my experience in working with individuals. In the past, in my work with folks with addictions, I have often focused on grieving the loss of the addicted self—of that person who used to be fun at parties or used to use drugs with their spouse. Suddenly that self ceases to exist, and the new self, that often loses old friends, spouses, or other things, emerges.

There are brain changes that occur during grief, and new brain patterns that need to be trained.[5] Grief may cause, directly

3. Schimelpfening, "Grief vs. Depression," sec. 2.
4. "Types of Grief and Loss," sec.1–5.
5. Shulman, "Healing Your Brain after Loss," sec. 1–3.

or indirectly, high blood pressure and compromised immunity.[6] New social networks can be formed, and old school "talking it through" and writing down feelings and thoughts can be definite tools. Here, however, you might be surprised by what I say next. That is, that in this instance, turning to God seems like a completely appropriate response. Loss changes balance, and sometimes that might make you question your place in the world. I think religion can help answer that question when nothing else seems to.

Anthony

I think I see a pattern here which may be a blessing for the sake of this book. It may be a result of our differences in personalities as referenced in other chapters. I tend to focus on most things in the more extreme, while Eric focuses on the more common aspects. It is my hope that this contrast will provide a broader range of perspectives on various levels.

For some people, feelings of loss are debilitating and don't improve even after time passes. This is known as complicated grief, sometimes called persistent complex bereavement disorder. In complicated grief, painful emotions are so long-lasting and severe that a person has trouble recovering from the loss and resuming his or her own life.

Different people follow different paths through the grieving experience. The order and timing of these phases may vary from person to person:

- Accepting the reality of the loss
- Allowing oneself to experience the pain of the loss
- Adjusting to a new reality in which the deceased is no longer present
- Having other relationships

If you're unable to move through these stages after more than a year after the death of a loved one, you may have complicated

6. Hairston, "How Grief Shows up in Your Body," sec. 1–2.

grief. If so, seek treatment.[7] As many of us have experienced the grief from losing a loved one, I once again have to contrast the different responses I experienced in the loss of both of my parents. I'm also hoping to illustrate the difference between facing adversity with faith in God and without.

I lost my father back in 1998. He was in Florida, and I was in New York City. At that time I had no faith; in fact, I had about as minimal interaction with God as possible. I was consumed with drinking, getting the next promotion, womanizing, and basically attempting to fill what I now know as "a God-shaped hole" with anything but God.

Upon receiving the horrible news about my dad, I was completely devastated and didn't know how to handle the grief that followed. I remember going to Florida for the first of two services, one in Florida and the other service where we grew up in Connecticut.

I remember being in a mall and feeling physically sick from this incredible grief that hit me like a freight train. At that time, I had no relationship with my Heavenly Father to fall back on or hold onto for strength. For years my dad was far more to me than just a dad; he had always been an extremely close, best friend. The thought of not being able to call my dad or to hear his voice again—ever—brought on an unbearable, immediate sorrow that was just seemingly unending.

After the funeral service in Connecticut, I drove back to New York City and went right back to work trying to bury the pain by staying extremely busy, but it relentlessly hung its gnawing self over me. The inner pain would take a long time to heal, and I relied on the only thing I knew that would somewhat numb the pain—excessive drinking.

In 2012, I lost my mother. At that time, I had a much stronger faith and the belief that she was now in perfect peace. The first day was difficult, but I looked at it from a completely different perspective. I knew that she was in the loving arms of our Heavenly Father. I knew she was free from any of this world's pain and was reunited with my dad and my loving grandparents. I knew I would one day

7. "Complicated grief symptoms and causes," para. 2–4.

be with her again. This verse from the apostle John in Revelation 21:4 (NKJ) also provided much comfort and reassurance: *"And God will wipe away every tear from their eyes; there shall be no more death, nor sorrow, nor crying. There shall be no more pain, for the former things have passed away."*

My faith in God made all the difference in my being able to accept the death of my mother and move through the stages associated with grief and loss. God lovingly carried me through the storm.

Eric

Anthony has struck upon something that bears repetition. He is astutely aware that in this process our conversation is with each other but also with those individuals who might choose to read these pages. Some will be in crisis; others will just be curious. We are not sure who those people will be, but I anticipate that many people might be interested in our perspectives on these obstacles we discuss as they relate to everyday life, as well as to those times when we find ourselves in crisis. For Anthony, crisis or not, he speaks to people who he hopes will seek or strengthen a relationship with God. For me, I speak to people as if to say that all of the obstacles we face are normal, that we all go through these things, and there are things we can do in therapy, and things we can do outside of therapy. Crisis is not always a part of seeking to better ourselves, nor should stress be the only motivator to explore and understand those feelings and emotions that drive us, for better or for worse. Grief, as an example, is a matter of degrees, and no one can know what level of crisis is created by a single event or what the recovery will look like. We can only know that whatever it is, we can handle it, whether with God's help, a therapist's help, or maybe just a good conversation with a friend.

Chapter 10

Gratitude

Anthony

GRATITUDE: "THE QUALITY OF being thankful; readiness to show appreciation for and to return kindness."[1] "Readiness to show appreciation," wow, what a concept! As previously mentioned, regarding the topic of forgiveness, there was a time in my life when not only forgiveness was in short supply, but gratitude was also not part of the equation. Let's just say expressing gratitude was not very high on the priority list. I was not only a part of this competitive and aggressive new work environment of Manhattan; I began to thrive in it. Seems like a lifetime ago when I was consumed by a culture that was the exact opposite of the definition of gratitude given above. From a broader perspective, it was the opposite of God's will. I was operating out of spiritual alignment, so to speak. These words gratitude, kindness, and forgiveness, and the act of demonstrating these qualities, was considered a sure sign of weakness.

Contrary to a readiness to show appreciation at that time, I always felt the need to be ready to respond to unkindness or the

1. "Gratitude."

next workplace political attack. I was living in a place of little gratitude and even less kindness. Why the change of heart? Perhaps a better question is, how did the heart change? The answer at its core is rather simple, but at the time seemed impossible.

My life became a complete disaster. Major resentments, hatred, regrets, selfishness, and anger led to major depression and its horrendous sidekick anxiety. If there is a level far below the "rock bottom stage of misery" that many people reference, I was even lower than that place.

When a person is consumed with this kind of emotional torment, looking for a way out of the misery is a paramount priority. Alcohol and gambling became my escape from reality. The problem was, these things only became sources of even more pain and destruction, not to mention my waking up each day with the original misery, which I desperately tried to keep at bay during the illusion of drunkenness and a high limit casino gambler.

I believe it's often difficult to appreciate what we have until we start losing things—big and little things and even many of the things in between. It was in this dark place where my heart was positioned to be transformed by the great physician Himself, my Lord and Savior Jesus Christ.

Let me start with this important point: God gets the glory for all of what comes next. All of these things are a result of His love, grace, mercy, and transforming power. In our weakness He becomes our strength during the storms of life. You may be saying, what does this transformation of the heart even mean? What does that look like?

The transformation makes itself apparent when someone who is far from perfect—someone who the majority of people who ever met this person would never think that he or she would ever mention God, Jesus, or the Bible—suddenly desires to serve God and is not afraid to tell people about Him. Yes, God is in the business of restoring hearts and lives.

I have been so blessed to witness God performing this transformation of the heart, not only in myself, but also in hundreds of others at Banyan's Faith in Recovery program. I have seen people come in with zero gratitude and leave with incredible gratitude and newly found hope. Being a part of these experiences reinforces and increases my faith in God every time.

People truly can find hope in the hopelessness.

What does it mean? It means having an appreciation and being genuinely grateful for being pulled from the depths of despair. Not only that, but God continues to use me to encourage and provide hope to others who are going through the similar pain that I experienced.

Psalm 40:1 (NLT) sums it up far better than I can: *"He lifted me out of the pit of despair, out of the mud and the mire. He set my feet on solid ground and steadied me as I walked along."*

Notice how God doesn't just lift us out of the pit of despair; He steadies us as we walk through this life. I think of a father the first time his son is riding the bike without the training wheels. He doesn't just let him go; he steadies him as the son begins to balance himself on his new journey. When the son inevitably falls, the father is right there to pick him up.

I am also truly grateful for honorable men such as Joe Tuttle, Banyan's founder & CEO and Eric Oakes, Executive VP & COO who took a chance on me back in 2015. These two men took a leap of faith to start a Christian faith-based program when Banyan was in its fledgling state with only one Banyan location. Six years later we now have fourteen centers and recently expanded our Faith in Recovery program into all fourteen centers nationally at all levels of care.

I think the only way you cannot be overflowing with gratitude is if you choose to not focus on the obvious blessings. I believe it's a matter of cultivating a grateful heart. I am, as all of us are, still a work in progress, but the complete selfishness, depression, anxiety, resentments, and pursuit of worldly pleasures have been removed from my heart, and God replaced those negatives with gratitude and compassion for others who are broken in spirit and feeling hopeless. He can do the same for you!

The apostle Paul who experienced incredible suffering wrote this beautiful passage from prison. Consider Philippians 4:12,13

(NIV) *"I know what it is to be in need, and I know what it is to have plenty. I have learned the secret of being content in any and every situation, whether well fed or hungry, whether living in plenty or in want. I can do all this through Him who gives me strength."*

Eric

It is hard to argue that these powerful messages are not moving or cathartic! Anthony's passion is resonant in the words on the page, and the gratitude is the gift that comes out of it all! Yes, it would be difficult to argue, and I am not going to. Gratitude can be powerful, passionate, and most of all, infectious! So why do some of us seem to have such a hard time feeling or expressing gratitude? Turns out, there are reasons we may not commonly consider.

By now, anyone reading this has come to understand that I see it as my job to try to make a logical argument for emotions and feelings. By doing so, and perhaps demystifying them in that way, I hope that it will then seem more logical to address, rather than just accept, those emotional obstacles that stand in your way. On the subject of gratitude, the point could not be clearer. Being grateful, acting grateful, practicing gratitude, can directly and positively impact virtually every part of your life. Gratitude works positively on your emotional health, and on that of those around you, as well.

There is a surprising amount of literature and research on gratitude, the neuroscience of how gratitude changes the brain chemistry, and how many things are affected by practicing gratitude. It has been established in various studies that gratitude, as a feeling, comes from a particular part of the brain, the right anterior temporal cortex, and that some people have a greater development of that area than others. To answer my earlier question, it seems that gratitude then may come easier to some than to others. I think we all know that some people seem to be more "glass half-full" kind of people, but it seems that the construction of the brain may play a bigger role in that. We know that we can train our brains, so continuing to practice gratitude will make us better at it, and it will come more naturally.[2]

It is also in the research that practicing gratitude accounts for reduced depressive symptoms, anxiety, and stress. Gratitude has been shown to impact sleep, pain, and has even been credited with creating an increase in happiness, in ourselves and others. So, gratitude has the pay-it-forward capacity to change, not just yourself, but others as well. Again, the research is clear that showing your appreciation for others has a positive impact on intimate relationships, friendships, and social networks.[3]

So, I have repeatedly referenced gratitude as something to practice. It would be easy to think of gratitude as a simple reaction to an event. Someone gives you a gift, and you are grateful, and you say, "thank you," and everyone feels better. But I would suggest that it rarely works that way. In fact, when you think about it, much of what people do may not even register on your radar. In 2018, AJ Jacobs wrote about his experience in combatting his normally less thoughtful approach to others to track down everyone involved in his morning cup of coffee. From the barista to the supplier, to the growers of beans in Columbia, he deliberately visited and thanked them all.[4] This powerful exercise points to how much we are missing in our exploration of gratitude, and how purposeful we sometimes have to be in order to truly live in gratitude. Practicing gratitude is necessary because the feeling or idea may not be self-revealing. This practice may require you to stop and inventory your day to think about who or what has positively impacted it, then take a moment to feel grateful.

Years ago, there was a man who worked in my charge in the maintenance department at a center I was directing. He had a crew of four or five under him, but the turnover in his department was continuous. The constant theme amongst the departing staff was that they felt under appreciated. I met with this supervisor one

2. Chowdhury, "The Neuroscience of Gratitude and How It Affects Anxiety & Grief," para. 14.

3. Ackerman, "28 Benefits of Gratitude," sec. 1–2.

4. Schilling, "A.J. Jacobs Loved His Morning Coffee," para. 2.

day, and he expressed frustration that he was losing so many good employees. I asked him, "Do you tell them they are doing a good job?" And his answer was shocking to me. He stated, "Absolutely not! My father taught me never to tell someone they are doing a good job, because then they will stop trying so hard!" This simple inability to acknowledge and express gratitude clearly impacted the supervisor and employees alike and had tremendous negative impact on the company as well.

In my own life I have tried in the past few years to express gratitude when I can. I can be a cynical guy sometimes. Despite this, I try to embrace feeling lucky, instead of waiting for the other shoe to drop, as it were. Still, I miss so many opportunities to express gratitude. Recently, I almost lost a colleague and friend who expressed to me that he felt undervalued. It was true that I had neglected to say thanks for his work or, and more importantly, his friendship. While it is true that my life, no different than most, has many negative events in it, it is equally true that I have an abundance of good fortune. Depending on the obstacles faced on a particular day, gratitude may begin with just being grateful for breathing. But with practice, a list of a thousand things can begin to take focus. I don't think it comes naturally to my brain. The crazy part is that gratitude is like a superfood. It is packed with benefits for your health and wellbeing. We know that it impacts everything from depression and suicide to marriage and productivity. So, I need to add more of it to my daily diet and start reaping the rewards.

A couple years ago something extraordinary happened to me in a checkout line in Walmart. I was there to pick up a few grocery items that were left out of our weekly shopping, so I had a handful of things in a basket. As I approached the checkout, I lined up behind another shopper, a smartly dressed, middle-aged woman. As she finished laying her items out on the belt, she motioned toward my basket, and said to the associate, ". . . and I will be purchasing his items as well today." I was stunned, and, of course, protested. The woman was kind and firm, and simply said, "I am fortunate."

That was it. Her motive was not bigger or smaller than that, to the best of my knowledge.

I was so moved by that gesture that I have begun to replicate it. Perhaps once a month, I look behind me in a checkout line and surprise that person with a random act of kindness. I believe in my own mind that this might be a better use of my money and time than any organized charity, because it really gets to the heart of it all. If you have gratitude, share it.

Anthony

I believe Eric captures the essence of gratitude with the below point:

"So, practice is necessary because the feeling or idea may not be self-revealing. It may require you to stop and inventory your day to think about who or what has positively impacted it, then take a moment to feel grateful." The blueprint for gratitude is right there for the taking: practice + inventory your day + think or focus on who or what positively impacted it = Gratitude.

Consider what the apostle Paul wrote in Philippians 4:8 (NIV). Let's keep in mind as previously mentioned, Paul wrote Philippians from prison. To put this in perspective, the first century prisons were not furnished with TV's and ping pong tables, but far worse in many respects, yet he wrote what is arguably one of the most uplifting books in all of the Bible. *"Finally, brothers and sisters, whatever is true, whatever is noble, whatever is right, whatever is pure, whatever is lovely, whatever is admirable—if anything is excellent or praiseworthy—think about such things."*

Paul was driving home the point of transforming our negative thoughts to the good things happening in life. Think of it as minimizing something on your computer. It's still there; you can always go back to the pain and aggravation if, for whatever reason, you'd ever want to do that. Speaking of computers, I have yet to come across a screen saver displaying a horrible scene or tragic accident. I think there's a lesson in this. The screen saver almost always highlights something beautiful or meaningful to us. Basically, this is what Paul desperately tried to convey to us from prison in writing Philippians 4:8. So, if this is the case, why are we minimizing the good things and highlighting the negative in our thoughts?

I'll close with this: If you have ever watched the news on television, you may have noticed during the sportscast there is something called the "highlight reel" where they show you the great plays that occurred during a game. We all know there were bad plays, bad coaching decisions, etc., too, but that's not the focus nor should it be.

I'm not minimizing this by any means. For years, as I have mentioned in other chapters, I was relentlessly tormented to the core by my own thoughts for long periods of time. I learned the hard way, but in the process, I gained an intimate understanding of how detrimental focusing on the negative aspects of life can be. Focusing on the negative is the opposite of genuinely recognizing and expressing appreciation and gratitude. Life is not a dress rehearsal. We simply don't know how much longer we have here, so let's make every effort to live in state of gratitude.

Chapter 11

Anxiety

Anthony

"Peace I leave with you; my peace I give you. I do not give to you as the world gives. Do not let your hearts be troubled and do not be afraid." John 14:27 (NKJ)

You may have heard this Bible verse or at least the first half of it toward the end of a church service. The only reason I was familiar with it while growing up was it alerted me that the church service was almost over. Maybe you can relate and didn't have much of a choice in attending church services either.

The priest would say the first half of the verse, which for many years I didn't even know was a Bible verse. He would then direct us to shake hands (pre-Covid, of course) with people who were sitting near us as a kind, peaceful gesture. This was followed by communion, and then the priest would say the only words I really wanted to hear: "The mass has ended. Go in peace."

Today that same verse means so much more! Jesus was emphasizing that His peace is far different than the so-called peace that the world has to offer us. The happiness or peace that the world has to offer is temporary. Worldly peace fluctuates as our daily circumstances change, sometimes within a matter of minutes. We receive good news that brings us happiness . . . then the discouraging news! It's as if this worldly peace quickly evaporates.

Many people never find true peace because the peace of Jesus is a byproduct of having an intimate relationship with God the Father through Christ the Son, not just the vain interaction of calling on Him when we are in trouble.

Maybe you know people in your life who only reach out to you when they need something. You may reluctantly help them each time, but it's more transactional and impersonal than relational. There is no deep, personal relationship because you and are simply going through the motions and not seeking anything of substance. You may even accommodate the need in order to avoid the guilt that follows if you don't answer their call. Why would we ever do this with our Creator who wants desperately to communicate with us to show us how to navigate this life without being consumed with anxiety.

It's something maybe you wrestle with yourself. Sure, you believe that God exists and maybe He even loves you, but you don't want to relinquish control or give Him the wheel. It's more of this type of thing: "God, I'll drive, and you sit in the back seat" approach. "If I get lost, I'll let you know." The more we try to control things, the more we open the door for anxiety and worry to emerge in our lives. The more I tried to take full control of the wheel, the more often I ended up lost in life.

If you travel in faith circles, you'll hear about the emptiness that is felt by someone who doesn't know God yet, only knows about Him. This emptiness is described as a "God-shaped hole." Everyone tries very hard to fill this "God-shaped hole" to appease the gnawing, inner void within us. We try with all kinds of things to fill the void: money, success, material things, people, alcohol, substances, gambling, and many other things, but nothing completely satisfies us long-term. We find ourselves empty again, ready to grab onto anything else that catches our eye as something we think we need to reduce or keep the anxiety and emptiness at bay.

This is not to minimize all the anxiety-producing things that are taking place in the world. We are all going to have things to be concerned about, but concern is something we control. Anxiety and worry can control us. The more we surrender our will to His will, the less we have to be anxious about in life.

Eric

As with most of the subjects we have discussed thus far, we really have to start with some distinctions. Anxiety is something that we all experience to some degree. Anxiety disorders are a description of a host of experiences that are dysfunctional and sometimes debilitating. There can be a huge difference, both in the experience and how one approaches its management.

Anxiety can be good for us. Anxiety is a state of physiological heightened excitement. It can motivate us by giving us energy, help us concentrate, or help us generally persevere. It is normal to have anxiety before public speaking, a first date, your wedding, a test, or things like that. Your palms get sweaty, your heart races a little, and you can't seem to relax. In these cases, anxiety can keep you on your toes while you get through a stressful event.

We have already discussed anxiety disorders to some degree. Some of them are generalized anxiety disorders, panic attacks, and phobias. Each of these is characterized by such a level of anxiety that we engage in avoidant behavior to relieve them or we cannot experience them without negative consequence. For example, we might not be willing to drive for fear of having a panic attack while in traffic. If you have anxiety that doesn't seem to go away, or if anxiety is keeping you from enjoying life, then I recommend you seek professional help for an evaluation. In these cases, there are effective treatments that are evidence-based and vary from talk therapies to medications.

It is not completely clear what makes someone have anxiety or anxiety disorders. Stress plays a part, and family history or genetic links may be factors. It is established that caffeine, alcohol, and other chemicals can play a role as well. Sometimes anxiety stands alone, and sometimes it is more likely a symptom of something else.[1]

So, let's talk about the non-disorder-level anxiety—stuff we all feel. I would posit that anxiety for me is decreased when I add two components. The first is that I tell myself that there are certain things I cannot control. I often feel "out of control" when it is, in fact, the case. Take an exam, as an example. I can control how hard I study, but I cannot control the questions, the room, the atmosphere, or the mood of the professor who will be grading my responses. Anxiety, then, can be greatly reduced when I realize that not all the outcome of an event is up to me, and, therefore, it's not all of my responsibility. Only my part is.

The next thing I tell myself is, "This too shall pass!" This familiar statement is no truer than when we are stressed and anxious about an event on our horizon. I often look at the clock and say to myself, "in 'x' number of days, hours, or minutes, this will be a thing of the past," and there will no longer be anything to control. This is liberating because it does what we have been talking about throughout; it creates a hope scenario! Hope is the belief that things will work out, that they will be different, or improve, or that something good is on the horizon. Without a belief that relief is possible, life would be difficult indeed.

Anthony's descriptions of normal attempts to relieve anxiety through drug or alcohol abuse, gambling, or achievement of wealth fit my understanding of the issues at hand. Many of us have tried those methods. Often, I believe they work for a while, but eventually they stop or make things worse. The alleviation through prayer or letting his God "take the wheel" makes perfect sense to me, given that it speaks directly to relinquishing the attempts at control of those things over which we have no control. If it works for you, then it is a brilliant strategy, but I think there will be times where you can benefit from other approaches. As Anthony states that he wishes not to diminish those who suffer, I think he understands that we risk oversimplification by offering any of these as the only coping skill. Throughout life, our stress levels and experience

1. "Anxiety," (*Medline*), sec. 1–8.

of anxiety may well change, and that may require different levels of intervention to meet the changing needs.

Here is another place where I advocate telling on yourself. If you are an "anxious person," you might have constant minor worries or thoughts that are difficult to shake. I know lots of people like that, and often they benefit from something as simple as checking with another person. I have a family member who regularly talks about their anxious thoughts and feelings, to which I respond with what I hope are reality-based or grounding statements. Sometimes things like pointing out the statistical likelihood that everything will be fine or even stating that a particular fear has little basis in reality helps them feel more grounded. The response to me is often, "I need you to tell me these things, and that's why I tell you what I am thinking."

Relaxation techniques and meditation are going to be of help to many, as they are readily available and are used by people in all corners of the globe. Lots of things can reduce anxiety, I think. However, anxiety is part of living, unless it sticks us stuck, making us unable to move forward. Then it's a part of all the junk we need to remove from our path. It's something we can do something about, although it is not likely going to go away completely. For me, anxiety is distinct from stress, in that I don't necessarily worry a lot, while I do certainly get feelings of pressure from stress. For others, it is a near constant voice. We just need to make sure hope is louder.

Anthony

Worry is synonymous with anxiety. The word worry in Greek, the language in which the New Testament was originally written, means "to go to pieces," "torn," and "pulled apart in different directions."[2]

Are you being pulled apart in different directions? Are you seeking human approval or God's approval? If we are aligning our decisions with God's will, the decisions are already made for us. Do we lie about something or tell the truth? Are we transparent and own up to a mistake or do we cover up our mistakes? You may

2. "Anxiety," (*Bible Hub*), see Greek ref #3309.

have heard the saying, "Oh, what a tangled web we weave . . . when first we practice to deceive."[3]

I believe often times when the anxiety is through the roof, it may have something to do with a decision we are in the process of making or not making. It may seem logical but just doesn't feel right. It's that persistent feeling that comes upon us, we may not understand it but we are aware of it. I believe that is the Spirit of God, the Holy Spirit who is leading us in the right direction, directing our path. That still small voice in our spirit. His conviction!

However, we have the gift of free will and could disregard this impression. I have done it many times, and every time I regret not listening to Him. Proverbs 3:5,6 (NKJ) provides some clarity on this. *"Trust in the Lord with all your heart, And lean not on your own understanding; In all your ways acknowledge Him, And He shall direct your paths."* What is our role in the passage? To trust. We don't need to know the details of Gods plan; we just need to trust that He has one.

The apostle Paul provides a good blueprint to stop worrying in order to find real peace in Philippians 4:6,7 (NLT)—*"Don't worry about anything; instead, pray about everything. Tell God what you need and thank him for all he has done. Then you will experience God's peace, which exceeds anything we can understand. His peace will guard your hearts and minds as you live in Christ Jesus."*

The word "then" is significant. It tells us that we play a role in this and what we can expect after we replace worrying with prayer. (Prayer should be *in place* of worry not *with* worry. If you are still worrying while or after you are praying, then keep on praying.)

Maybe you can relate to this. When I was suffering with tremendous anxiety over eight years ago, I read that passage many times, but I didn't apply it. I didn't do what Paul instructs us to do. I wasn't praying about the many issues that were tormenting me or thanking God for what He had done. When I finally began to apply this passage truly from my heart, things began to change for the better. James 1:22 (NIV) says, *"Do not merely listen to the word, and so deceive yourselves. Do what it says."*

3. Wise, "Oh What A Tangled Web," 1.

The reality is, you could listen to sermons for a lifetime, but until you actually apply those words to your life, in other words, do what they tell you to do, you will not see the incredible benefits that Jesus promises in Matthew 7:24–27 (NIV), *"Therefore, everyone who hears these words of mine and puts them into practice is like a wise man who built his house on the rock. The rain came down, the streams rose, and the winds blew and beat against that house; yet it did not fall, because it had its foundation on the rock. But everyone who hears these words of mine and does not put them into practice is like a foolish man who built his house on sand. The rain came down, the streams rose, and the winds blew and beat against that house, and it fell with a great crash."* A house built on sand is unstable and awaits destruction when the storm comes. We too have storms in life. What are we building our foundation on and who is designing our house?

Here is one final illustration on the application of the word of God in our life. Let's say someone gave you a book on how to get in shape because you agreed that you needed to do something about your poor physical condition. When you see that person a few months later, you are even more out of shape! When the person asks you if you read the book, your answer (assuming you're telling the truth and actually read the book . . .) will have to be, "Yes, I read it, but I didn't actually do anything it said!" The answers were right there, but they were not implemented.

None of the above mentioned in my section is to minimize any brain chemistry malfunctions that can also lead to the tremendous suffering which results from anxiety. This is what worked for me and many others who have come into our program at Banyan's Faith in Recovery program over the past six years. So, the next time you are tempted to worry, think of it as an open invitation God is giving you to pray.

Eric

There is going to be a common experience here that anyone reading will likely appreciate. In fact, some may be disappointed that it has not yet been directly addressed. Anxiety can often lead us to feeling overwhelmed. Overwhelming feelings are universal. We all have them. But what we do with them is what can change our lives. This feeling seems to shut us down and immobilize us. All of our circuits overload; we blow a fuse, our head goes in our hands, and we stare. We can't seem to move, and our mind races. It is extremely uncomfortable. This is actually your brain experiencing a threat and focusing on it.[4] The unfortunate part is what happens next. Most of us escape that feeling by avoiding it. We distract ourselves with something that takes our minds away. Today, that distraction is often in the predictable nonsense on social media, but is also TV, food, or emergency spot cleaning of that toaster that suddenly seems like it needs a good once over.

What this process does is useful in that it takes our brain out of crisis mode and moves it into a mode closer to relaxation. The fight or flight brain activity subsides. But then we typically reload the brain by doing the same thing over and over again, so the feeling of being overwhelmed returns. Then we internalize that cluster of feelings and ideas of being out of control yet again, believe we cannot function, and we continue in our avoidance behavior. It is important to take things in smaller chunks when these feelings are present. It is important to be mindful. Breathe deep and try to limit distractions. Suggestion: make a list, so that you don't have to keep running through it in your head. Do the first thing on your list, read one paragraph, make one bed, write one sentence, make one phone call. Then break, then repeat. You don't have to do it all at once, and when we try, we know we usually end up doing none of it. If we attack it in smaller pieces, it is easier to master, and mastery increases our sense of control. Anxiety decreases, and we feel less overwhelmed. Easier said than done, I am sure, but it's something we all experience and can overcome. As usual, there are degrees here, and therapy can help if feeling overwhelmed feels more like a way of life than an isolated event.

4. Amisha, "The Brain Science of Attention and Overwhelm," sec. 6,10.

Chapter 12

Trauma

Eric

I AM WHAT MOST would consider a decent swimmer. I grew up around water, and while I am no athlete, I spent a fair amount of time jumping off docks and playing games in neighbors' pools. Later in life, I used pools for exercise, doing laps in the gym a few times a week. So, ten years ago, when I grabbed a kayak and slid it into the lake at the cabin my family rented, I considered it nothing more than a reasonable way to spend a few minutes in nature. It was a beautiful cool day, and while the water was cold, the experience of being alone on the mirrored blue was mesmerizing. I did not think I needed the life jacket hanging on the dock, but threw it in the little hold on the bow anyway. Off I went. I didn't think it was important to mention my short trip out to my family who were inside preparing for dinner.

Thirty feet from shore, I stopped to look around me. It was beautiful. But I turned too fast, lost a little balance, and the kayak began to shimmy. I could not right it in time, and it turned over, and I was tossed underwater in a matter of seconds. Suddenly, when I quickly surfaced, I was confused, disoriented, and cold.

The thirty feet to shore was not far, but I couldn't decide whether I should try to swim or try to get back on the boat, and panic set in. I was alone. It was so quiet and calm, and so discordant with what was happening in my head. No one knew I was out there, and I was panicking. I was alone and I was cold. I started to thrash about, and eventually the thrashing got organized into a bodily effort at swimming, and I was on my way in to shore. Maybe a minute elapsed from capsize to first stroke toward safety, maybe less.

When I arrived on the edge, my wife happened to be outside, and when she saw me dragging my soaked self, my kayak, and life jacket to the sand, she laughed. What a sight I was from the outside! I joined her in laughing, and we told the kids about it, and they laughed too. I dried off and went about the rest of my day, with the occasional ribbing from the family about my "disaster at sea." The whole event was 5 minutes in length, at most, and was quickly filed away as a slight embarrassment and a bit of a failure—not my first and not my last. All good, I thought, until the nightmares that happened two nights later. I woke up to the feeling that I was trapped underwater and drowning. Woke up to sweats and heart pounding. It wasn't rational. I was never in real danger. I was not likely to actually drown that day. And yet, something was wrong that was starting to intrude into my life. It made me worry, and the fear of more nightmares caused anxiety. My wife is a psychologist, and I am a social worker, so we were able to talk together about this experience and call it what it was. Trauma. I can't say I would have always known that. In this experience, labeling it and talking through it made tremendous difference. I can still conjure the images, but it doesn't insert itself into my conscience.

Trauma usually shows up in intrusive thoughts or emotions or sudden recalls of events at unexpected times.[1] Trauma and PTSD are subjects that could fill entire tomes, so I cannot do them justice here. The trauma experience can cause nightmares and rapid heart rate, depressed feelings, anger, or trouble concentrating

---

1. Substance Abuse and Mental Health Services Administration, 33–52, 61–75.

amongst other things.[2] Trauma reactions over-activate the amyg-dala and hippocampus in the brain which causes a stress response and triggers memory formation.[3] For severe trauma, or PTSD, the trauma can feel as if it is being relived at the drop of a hat, triggered sometimes by even minor sounds, smells, words, or other events. Trauma, however, in all its forms, can be treated. In the past several decades, tremendous advancement in trauma therapy has reached more people, and trauma has become a more accepted part of the human experience. As an administrator, where once I, myself, was woefully ill-skilled to help trauma survivors, I now require all of my clinicians to be trained in trauma therapies, and each clinician has the skills necessary to address all types of traumas, including some of the most severe.

When I was first starting out in this field, I took a job work-ing with adolescents. I was young and inexperienced but felt that because I could relate to the angst of youth, I could be effective in the aid of pretty much all that ailed them. I could not have been, in fact, less prepared for some of the challenges in front of me had they been from another planet. One client, in particular, a teen-age girl, had been working with me for several weeks. Over those weeks she seemed to make significant progress in her day-to-day life, and we had processed many issues about her relationship to her parents, her peers, and her own feelings of self- worth. At least, I thought we had processed these, and that she had made progress. That was until one day she presented herself to me in hysterics. This young girl was nearly inconsolable, and it took all of my best that I could muster to calm her down. Once calm, it was clear there was more to this girl and her pain than what I understood. It was then that she, still shaking and quietly crying, described how she had been raped by an older boyfriend six months earlier. All of the progress she had made with me, she explained, had been a front, pretending to be better because she wanted to be better. But she, with just a few years of life in her rearview, realized she would not get better until she faced this hard truth—the truth that she had

2. "The Science behind Trauma," *Multiplying Connections*, sec 1,3.
3. DiLonardo, "What Are PTSD Triggers? "para 1–3.

been violently assaulted. This was trauma, a traumatic event that had been at the core of so much of her pain, and she knew that dealing with it was her best shot at moving forward.

The sad reality was that I was woefully unprepared to help this girl who had come to me. The fact was that in all of my training, some thirty-five years ago, trauma was only truly discussed in one context. Post-Traumatic Stress Disorder, or PTSD, was primarily the burden carried by a war time soldier. And then, it didn't really matter anyway, because I was essentially taught that trauma was too hard, too specialized, and too complicated for most of us clients and therapists alike. PTSD cases were to be put off until another time, referred to another therapist, or left untreated because it just wasn't necessary to force people through the pain it would take to face the trauma all over again. The conclusion of this story was that I do not know what became of that young girl over the years, but if she got the help she needed and desired, it wasn't because of me.

Today, clinicians recognize something much different. Yes, PTSD is still a very real concern, but it is not exclusive to the veteran. Anyone can suffer from its effects. Trauma is part of many people's experiences, and we are all vulnerable. Trauma is different for all of us, but it is always the result of the brain's reaction to something that doesn't make sense or something that cannot be processed in the way the brain perceives as a true threat to our safety.[4]

Traumatic events differ from person to person but can be just about anything. It is commonly understood that two people can witness the same event, and perhaps only one experiences the event as traumatic. Clinicians are trained to help navigate identification, processing, and healing from all types of traumas with a host of interventions. I earlier spoke of my own experience and spoke about talking it through. This is not always the best approach to wellness, and clinicians know how to distinguish that as well.

Trauma can vary in severity and can cause larger or smaller disruptions in someone's life. Many of us can, for example, conjure up a memory of a sad, scary, or uncomfortable event that still

4. Kraybill, "What is Trauma?" sec. 3–5.

causes us to have some of the same feelings emerge that were present on the day of the event. And we can probably vividly recall at least part of the event as if it were yesterday. This is trauma on a minor scale. But sometimes these "recalls" keep us avoiding situations. Perhaps we avoid the intersection where we had a fender bender because it still can remind us of that day and how we felt.

I believe that trauma and PTSD are often at the ground level of many of those things that bring us to therapy or cause disruption in our day-to-day lives. I believe that our brain attempts to protect us from events it does not think we can handle, and it sort of short-circuits in the process. In my treatment centers we now see trauma as something that likely will have to be addressed if someone is to really master a plan of drug-free recovery. The progress in this field of study however, has meant that hope is alive, and this is an obstacle that we can tackle together. For some of us, I doubt we have ever labeled our trauma as such. For others, we know something was traumatic, but are reticent to acknowledge it for fear of being seen as weak, or for being seen as invalidating to those who have experienced horrors in this this world. Who wants to compare their bee sting with someone else's story of being a hostage or being trapped in a burning building? We don't control our brain's interpretation of an event. We don't know why it happened; we just know that we can do something about it. Again, this is about hope, and in this case, freedom from things that have kept us back for too long.

Anthony

One of the objectives of this book as Eric wrote in the introduction: "The point of this book is to relate a conversation between two people who see things differently but are willing to talk about them. We wanted to create a safe place to talk about religion and social science, and to actually enter the space where they converge. We do this in the name of helping all people, not just the ones who agree with us."

Finding Hope in Hopelessness

As Eric and I write this chapter, it's one of the last chapters and it is another example of the point of the book, "Relate a conversation between two people who see things differently but are willing to talk about those things." In the process of listening to someone, you may not agree with them on many things, but if you keep listening, you may find that with some topics, you can't agree more. Such is the case with this topic of trauma.

I referenced our differences of opinions in a previous chapter. I mentioned how Eric often focuses more on the topics from more of a generalized view or how many of life's adversities are experiences which are common to a wide range of people. My viewpoint is often on the more extreme cases. When you work in the mental health and substance abuse industry, you encounter many people who are suffering with trauma often from their childhood who are sometimes in great need of hope. I'm sure there are others who never realize the source of their pain. Eric makes excellent points on how trauma and PSTD are not just experienced by our incredible combat veterans as many would think.

Eric's point that "we don't control our brain's interpretation of an event," so what may be traumatic to one person may not be to another. I believe we need to move away from the assumption that since someone experienced something that society does not consider traumatic, they must be simply weak-minded or attention-seeking. We must stop judging and stigmatizing people and start listening to them. This should apply to all mental health disorders, but especially with trauma. It may save lives.

Another aspect that I really love about this conversational format is hearing two different perspectives. Keeping that in mind, there will be some readers who are more receptive and familiar with the faith sections, while others are more receptive and familiar with the clinical.

It is our hope that people will read both. I'd like to reference a study conducted by Baylor University. As a chaplain and national faith director, I encounter people quite often who say they believe only what they can see. The opposite seems to occur with believers in God who say that they can "see" more clearly—what may not be easily visible to others—because of their faith and what the Bible has taught them. The Baylor study shows benefits of Bible-based trauma healing programs in prisons.

Inmates who participated in a Bible-based, trauma-healing ministry program showed enhanced emotional well-being and a significant decrease in the negative consequences of trauma, a recent study by the American Bible Society and Baylor University revealed. Through participating in "Healing the Wounded Heart," ABS Bible-based Correctional Trauma Healing Program participants experienced a decline in PTSD and vengefulness. Also, they experienced increases in forgiveness, resilience, and meaning in life.[5]

This is one of many studies which have revealed very positive results in impacting many lives. It brings us back to the opening of my section of this chapter. Let's do more listening to one another, and if something works for the betterment of those who are suffering, let's consider it, even if everyone may not be in complete agreement with the method.

In the book of James, chapter 1, verse 19 (NIV) we read, *"My dear brothers and sisters, take note of this: Everyone should be quick to listen, slow to speak, and slow to become angry."*

I don't know about you, but I wish I'd come across this verse and applied it to my own life years ago. Perhaps there are other verses such as this one that the inmates of the Baylor study incorporated into their own lives. So, whatever the case may be during the above study or the many others, I truly believe that the substance and mental health care system, as well as our amazing country, the United States of America, in general, could unite if we begin to be quick to listen, slow to speak, and slow to become angry!

Eric

I don't know why humans are subjected to a variety of experiences. I do know that I am fortunate to have such a life that has protected

5. "The Benefit of Bible-Based Trauma Healing," para. 1–2.

me from the unimaginable thus far. As such, I am less of an expert on trauma than others in my field.

A few years ago, my administrative work in one of our clinical buildings was disturbed by a client in the hallway. The young man, a twenty-five-year-old working on his heroin addiction, was screaming and banging walls, refusing to follow the clinic staff's best attempts at intervention. Somehow, we were able to usher the gentleman into my office, where he continued to act out, although in a somewhat diminished capacity. In short order, I was able to discern that his behavior was driven by lack of sleep and high anxiety. I do not recall much of the dialogue, but the catharsis of this event, this outpouring of emotion, culminated in his telling a story that he had never told another to that point. This young man revealed that he had, a few years earlier, been riding motorcycles in a mountainous area with his best friend. The man had secured heroin for both of them, and they had gotten high. They then proceeded to ride, and a resulting horrific crash caused this man, who had provided his friend with drugs, to witness his friend's death. This experience plagued him since then and was at the root of his inability to sleep, manage emotions, and function appropriately. Thankfully, this time around I was better prepared than the years-ago encounter with my young client, and I was able to help this gentleman work through his trauma with appropriate therapies, and he was able to gain increased peace and control over his life.

I generally agree with Anthony on the point that we are presenting two views, and I believe neither is the only possible truth. In the case above, I think this gentleman needed someone in the right place at the right time to help him work through his journey out of darkness. In keeping with both perspectives, I listened to this client, in the way we all need to listen better to each other.

Chapter 13

Self-Esteem

Eric

SELF-ESTEEM IS A BIG deal. It's a struggle to even start on this subject. It is so clear to me that low self-esteem is an obstacle that many must face when trying to push forward in this world. It is one of those things that sets the tone for how problems might be approached or how the world may be viewed. Like shame and the tapes we referenced elsewhere in this book, self-esteem is part of our makeup, our schema about ourselves, and the belief we hold in our abilities and potential.

Interestingly, clinical study has attempted over the years to pinpoint a solid definition of self-esteem, a solid source for its development, and grounded research about where it's located in the brain.[1] The simplest way to define self-esteem from my point of view is that self-esteem is our feeling of self-worth. But I think we can all relate to how it changes based on what is said or shown to us by parents and peers. So, I think it is a worth defined by perception. It is dramatically affected by what we believe people think of us, using scant specific data to draw larger conclusions. For example, if

1. "Self-Esteem Mapped in the Human Brain," para. 4–8.

one person says they don't like you, then you would assume that no one will ever like you. That one opinion has created a schema that you are unlikeable, and further that this is unlikely to change. Not a very hopeful scenario. Not a very truthful one either.

To add, then, it is unclear to the naked eye why some people who seem to have it all have low opinions of themselves, or low self-esteem, while others who seem to have very few resources or fortunes are apparently much more comfortable in their own skins. You and I would probably conjecture that our formative years have a lot to do with that. The messages our parents and friends send us in childhood matter. Genetics may also play a role.[2] Self-esteem also varies, as we travel through time and experience. Our self-esteem is certain to be higher on a day of a big success than it is on a day of a big disappointment.

Another way of looking at self-esteem is to measure personal efficacy or mastery. A belief that I can do something says that I believe in myself. The best place to form a belief that I can do something is in the aftermath of having accomplished a similar task. Building on success gives us more confidence in future success. Confidence is a huge weapon against fickle public opinion.

Where do we find hope? So, the hope is that things can turn around. Self-esteem is not fixed; it is moveable and constantly changing. More success, more positive feedback (from yourself and others), more acceptance, more motivation, and even more fun can all impact and change self-esteem. I believe that religious teaching will dictate that we take solace in God's love for us with all our faults. I believe that could certainly help, but that there are worldly activities that will strengthen our minds' defenses against our negative self-messaging.

Cognitive Behavioral Therapy, or CBT, is significantly focused on challenging our beliefs about how the world works and how we fit in it.[3] Therefore, it is a perfect fit for discussions about improving self-esteem. The big thing is that self-esteem is related directly to confidence. We need confidence to take a risk, and we

2. Cherry, "What Is Self-Esteem?" para. 2.
3. Cherry, "What Is Cognitive Behavior Therapy (CBT)?" para. 1–3.

need risk to get a reward. And what is confidence if it is not a mixture of hope and faith? Self-esteem fuels and feeds off the rest of the obstacles in our lives. It stands to reason that higher self-esteem would result in a higher belief in our ability to manage a crisis. This belief would lead to less depression, anxiety, and fear and would drive greater efficacy in addressing shame messages and even anger. More belief in yourself creates a greater willingness to take on more tasks with greater motivation.

There have been times in my life when a simple off-handed comment about my shirt or haircut could make or break my confidence. Many of us feel the sting of criticism and generalize it to our overall worth. The simple test for validity is empathy. How many times can you recall total rejection of another based on their clothing choice or hairstyle? It is unlikely that others have rejected you along with your shirt or a bad hair day, so why own it as truth in your own life? At the core of it we are social beings. We need each other and thrive in relationships. This understanding of how to navigate our sense of self becomes critical. For me, belief in myself and confidence waivers every day of my life. But over time, as I have matured and realized that I don't win every time, and that not everyone is going to like me, my self-esteem has become more stable and far more manageable.

In my business, nothing is more apparent than the cycle I have attempted to describe above. Day after day, individuals ravaged by substance abuse enter treatment at my facilities with low self-esteem. After months or years or even a lifetime of placing little value on themselves and placing drugs over safety, many believe the narrative they have written. They believe that they are not even worthy of basic care. But over time, we challenge this narrative. We work together on establishing efficacy and mastery over basic tasks. We treat the rest of the body to restore physical health, and we support the idea that no one is alone, and that no one should be left behind. The result is renewed, or perhaps newly discovered, belief in the self and desire to change. We treat doctors, lawyers, athletes, bankers, veterans, waitstaff, indigent folks, and celebrities. No one is immune, and no one is without the ability to change. Many individuals leave treatment feeling hopeful and worthy of success as they define it.

Self-esteem may well be the thread that ties all of this together. It can be the cause, the cure, the result, or the goal. I tend to look at it as more of a barometer. Levels of belief in oneself, feelings of worth, and mastery of tasks may well be both a symptom of the problem and a predictor of the work ahead.

Anthony

"People look at the outward appearance, but the Lord looks at the heart," 1 Samuel 16:7 (NLT) How might this relate to self-esteem?

Samuel was an Old Testament prophet who came to David's father Jessie to anoint the next king of Israel. David had seven older brothers who were battle-hardened military men with a lot of experience, so it was only natural that their father Jessie would assume that Samuel came to anoint one of his older sons when Jessie paraded his sons out to meet the prophet. However, it wasn't any of those sons that God wanted to anoint as the king.

David who was a young shepherd boy was not even considered. (That could do a number on someone's self-esteem.) Maybe you could relate to not even being considered during times of your life. I know I can relate.

If you know the rest of the story, you know that David went on to become a great king of Israel. He wrote half the Psalms and was one of the key figures in the Bible. So why didn't his father even consider him?

The verse above spells it out for us. David's father Jessie was looking at the outward appearance of his sons, not their hearts. How many times have we done the same when we first met someone? We may have quickly judged the person by a preconceived opinion and were later proven to be completely wrong! They may even end up to be one of our closest of friends.

As Eric referenced above, "The messages our parents and friends send us in childhood matter." In particular, when we are growing up and often yearning for our dad's approval, the words we receive can build us up or tear us down. If this applies to you, perhaps begin to look at it from this perspective. No one can make you feel inferior without your consent.[4]

Eric also made the strong point of how low self-esteem relates to those who are in treatment for substance use and or mental health disorders. They are beaten down by others' opinions and their own horrible opinions of themselves. It's as though society has cast its verdict, and the gavel has dropped, so to speak.

In our Faith in Recovery program, what I see oftentimes as the most destructive disposition to anyone's healthy self-esteem is a distorted view of how God sees them. They are convinced that they've crossed the line with God and are way too far gone for Him to want anything to do with them. It is a sense of shame that oftentimes far outweighs all else.

When they begin to realize that their identity is not based on what other people think of them or on their own low opinion of themselves, but how God really sees them, that is usually when a glimmer of hope shines in their eyes. They begin to accept what matters most is how God sees them, and that they are still loved by Him. He still has a plan and purpose for their lives, and they are fully understood. There isn't anything God doesn't already know about their past. I think it doesn't get any more hopeful than that! It is truly an adventure to witness God's redemptive power on full display at Banyan's Faith in Recovery program.

From a faith-based perspective, we focus on seeking God's approval, not on human approval. If you find yourself continually seeking human approval, you will miss discovering your true value and what God has for you. Trying to find self-validation through pleasing people is a slippery slope to navigate. People-pleasing sets us up for disappointment in ourselves and in others. What may be pleasing to someone one day may be the exact opposite the next day. God doesn't change, and He will not undermine His own principles. Hebrews 13:8 (NIV) *"Jesus Christ is the same yesterday and today and forever."* It really simplifies things when you have an audience of one and He is your greatest encourager.

4. Chery, "What does the Bible say about self-worth?" para. 1–3.

Psalm 117 is the shortest chapter in the Bible. Psalm 119 is the longest. Psalm 118 is the exact middle chapter of the Bible; there are 594 chapters before and 594 chapters after Psalm 118. Psalm 118:8 is the exact middle verse of the Bible. Does this verse say something significant about God's perfect plan for our lives? *"It's better to trust in the Lord than to put confidence in man."* Psalm 118:8 (NIV) Isn't it odd how this worked out, or is God in the center of it? The next time someone says they would like to find God's perfect will for their lives, just send them to the center of His word.[5]

5. "Bible Facts," sec. 2.

Chapter 14

Conclusion

Closing Thoughts

Eric

WE BEGAN THIS BOOK with three intentions. We wanted to lay out two different and sometimes opposing viewpoints, while still remaining friends. We wanted to talk about things that were common to others, in an attempt to help people. Finally, we wanted to show some of the many ways that hope perseveres and thrives. Hope, after all, is what everyone needs, and so many struggle to find it.

Since we began writing, the world around us continues to push down. The pundits on TV would have us believe that every day we are closer to the brink of total destruction. Perhaps we are, but Anthony and I don't think so. We think that as long as we can listen, talk, and put the work in, there is hope. We have discussed all manner of mental health issues and human concepts like forgiveness, anxiety, and gratitude, but what we haven't really spent much time on is the human capacity for compassion. Compassion will bring us where we need to be, if we are willing to allow it to enter the dynamic.

In this book we shared facts, science, beliefs, convictions, and vulnerability, and in so doing, we hoped to show compassion for each other and the reader. We looked at things the way we saw them but had respect for others as well. I hope that if one of us withdrew and were replaced, the outcome of presenting our beliefs, finding commonality, agreeing to disagree, and remaining motivated, optimistic, and hopeful, would be the same. We also talked about serious issues that many of us face when we are at home alone with ourselves or that those we love might also be facing. We believe that we have given you something to think about here too. We hope so.

As we finish this discussion, I cannot have a greater wish than to wish that our conversations would be the beginning of many others. I would like to think that we are all capable of having dialogues and disagreements. It so happens that Anthony and I differ in some conventional ways—religion, politics, lifestyle—even our writing and communication styles are polar. So, what if our contrasts were different? What if our positions were different because we did not share race, or gender, or country of origin? Our opinions would not be the same, but I hope our process would be.

Anthony

Numerous references have been made of people throughout the Bible whose hearts and minds were transformed and renewed by God. He then proceeded to use them in mighty ways to impact the world. The apostle Paul would be the best example. The Saul to Paul transformation! A man who was extremely passionate in his beliefs and world views, but something dramatically changed along his journey on the road to Damascus. The Lord showed up! These beautiful transformations are still happening today as referenced in the Bible.

We witness true change in those who enter the doors of Banyan's Faith in Recovery program. People are often in a state of complete hopelessness. Then something dramatically changes. The Lord shows up!

Conclusion

If the conversational approach in our book sparks any broader discussions with people who are on opposite ends of the spectrum and dug in on their various positions, it was well worth the effort.

Our incredible country is more divided than many of us can remember. Eric and I wholeheartedly believe there is still hope for people to agree to disagree and move past their differences of opinions, that good can truly come out of bad situations, and people can still find hope in hopelessness.

Bibliography

"About Amber Alert." *U.S. Department of Justice/ Office of Justice Programs.* October 20, 2019. https://amberalert.ojp.gov/faqs.

Ackerman, Courtney. "28 Benefits of Gratitude & Most Significant Research Findings." *Positive Psychology.* 5 Feb. 2022. https://positivepsychology. com/benefits-gratitude-research-questions/.

"Addiction is a Stronghold." *New Life Spirit Recovery Treatment Center.* Blog. https://newlifespiritrecovery.com/addiction-is-a-stronghold-but-what-does-that-mean/.

American Psychiatric Association: Diagnostic and Statistical Manual of Mental Disorders. Fifth Edition. (DSM-5) Arlington VA. 2013. 155.

Amisha, Jha. "The Brain Science of Attention and Overwhelm." *Breathwork-Science.* https://breathwork-science.org/2020/11/03/the-brain-science-of-attention-and-overwhelm/. November 3, 2020.

"Anger, Hostility, and Violent Behavior." *Michigan Medicine.* 26 February 2020. https://www.uofmhealth.org/health-library/anger.

"Anxiety." *Bible Hub.* Helps Word Studies *Strong's Greek Concordance.* 2021 https://www.biblehub.com/greek/3309.htm.

"Anxiety." *MedlinePlus.* National Institute of Mental Health. 20 September 2021. https://medlineplus.gov/anxiety.html.

"Anxiety Disorders." *U.S. Department of Health and Human Services.* National Institute of Mental Health. https://www.nimh.nih.gov/health/topics/anxiety-disorders.

Ardito, Rita B, and Daniela Rabellino. "Therapeutic alliance and outcome of psychotherapy: historical excursus, measurements, and prospects for research." *Frontiers in Psychology.* vol. 2 270. 18 Oct. 2011. doi:10.3389/fpsyg.2011.00270.

Bibliography

"The Benefit of Bible-Based Trauma Healing Program." American Bible Society. https://www.prnewswire.com/news-releases/american-bible-society-and-baylor-university-study-shows-the-benefit-of-bible-based-trauma-healing-program-301257945.html.

"Bible and the 12 Steps." *The 12 Steps of Recovery.* November 2020. https://12Step.org/references/bible.

"Bible Facts." *His Kingdom Prophecy.* March 21, 2011. https://www.hiskingdomprophecy.com/bible-facts/.

Bradshaw, John. *Healing the Shame That Binds You.* 1988. Deerfield Beach, Florida. Health Communications.

Brazier, Yvette. "Everything You Need to Know about Phobias." *Medical News Today.* Updated Nov 26, 2020. https://www.medicalnewstoday.com/articles/249347.

Castella, Tom. "Luis Suarez: Does Anger Management Actually Work?" *BBC News Magazine.* 23 Apr. 2013. https://www.bbc.com/news/magazine-22264123.

Cherry, Kendra. "What Is Self-Esteem?" *Verywell Mind.* Updated 24 Apr. 2021. https://www.verywellmind.com/what-is-self-esteem-2795868.

Cherry, Kendra. "What Is Cognitive Behavior Therapy (CBT)?" *Verywell Mind.* Updated November 05, 2021. https://www.verywellmind.com/what-is-cognitive-behavior-therapy-2795747.

Chery, Fritz. "What does the Bible Say about self-worth?" *Bible Reasons* https://https://www.biblereasons.com/self-worth-and-self-esteem/. February 7, 2022.

Chowdhury, Madhuleena Roy. "The Neuroscience of Gratitude and How It Affects Anxiety and Grief." *Positive Psychology.* https://www.positivepsychology.com/neuroscience-of-gratitude/. February 2022.

Cohen, Adam. "Research on the Science of Forgiveness: An Annotated Bibliography." *Greater Good Magazine.* 2020. https://greatergood.berkeley.edu/article/item/the-science-of-forgiveness-an-annotated-bibliography. October 1, 2004.

"Complicated grief symptoms and causes." *Mayo Clinic.* 3 February 2022 https://mayoclinic.org/diseases-conditions/complicated-grief/symptoms-causes/syc-20360374.

Davis, Shanna. "Jargon Genesis: Think Outside the Box." *News St. Thomas Education.* https://www.news.stthomas.edu/jargon-genesis-think-outside-the-box/ June 03, 2010.

DiLonardo, Mary Jo. "What Are PTSD Triggers?" *WebMD.* 11 September 2001. https://www.webmd.com/mental-health/what-are-ptsd-triggers.

Dunne, Chris. "35 Best Teamwork Quotes to Inspire Collaboration." *Tameday.* Blog. https://www.tameday.com/teamwork-quotes/ July 5, 2019. #4.

"Fear." *Collins Dictionary.* https://www.collinsdictionary.com/us/fear.

Fraser, J. Scott. "Hope: A Foundation of All Psychotherapy That Works." *Psychology Today.* https://www.psychologytoday.com/ca/blog/breaking-the-cycle/201906/hope-foundation-all-psychotherapy-works.

Bibliography

Frysh, Paul. "Paranoia." *WebMD.* Medically Reviewed by Jennifer Casarella on September 09, 2021. https://www.webmd.com/mental-health/why-paranoid.

Gifford, Sheyna, et al. "The Intersection of Technology, Innovation and Creativity." *Now.* https://now.northrupgrumman.com/diversity-and-inclusion-create-better-outcomes-a-look-at-the-science/.

"Gratitude." *Lexico.* https://www.lexico.com/en/definition/gratitude.

Hairston, Stephanie. "How Grief Shows up in Your Body." *WebMD* archives. https:///www.webmd.com/special-reports/grief-stages/20190711/how-grief-affects-your-body-and-mind. July 11, 2019.

Hartney, Elizabeth. "What is Motivational Interviewing?" *Verywell Mind.* 30 May 2021. https://www.verywellmind.com/what-is-motivational-interviewing-22378.

"Hope." *Mirriam-Webster.* https://www.mirriam-webster.com/dictionary/hope.

Horvath, Tom. *Practical Recovery.* https://www.practicalrecovery.com/message-from-founder/.

Kahn, April. "What's Causing My Agitation?" *Healthline.* 11 February 2022https://www.healthline.com/health/agitation#diagnosis

Kraybill, Odelya. *Expressive Trauma Integration.* "What is Trauma?" *Psychology Today.* 31 January 2019. https://www.psychologytoday.com/us/blog/expressive-trauma-integration/201901/what-is-trauma

Kübler-Ross, Elisabeth and Ira Byock. *On Death & Dying: What the Dying Have to Teach Doctors, Nurses, Clergy & Their Own Families.* Scribner. 2019.

Mastroianni, Brian. "More Stressed than Ever since COVID-19 Started? You're Not Alone." 27 January 2022. https://salesjobinfo.com/more-stressed-than-ever-since-covid-19-started-youre-not-alone/.

McVean, Ada. "It's Time to Let the Five Stages of Grief Die." *Office for Science and Society.* 2 June 2019. https://www.mcgill.ca/oss/article/health-history/its-time-let-five-stages-grief-die.

Mothers Against Drunk Driving (MADD). "About Us: Mission & History." *MADD.* 2021, https://www.madd.org

Naspretto, Alicia. "CDC Fentanyl Overdoses." *Above Top Secret.* Blog. Updated December 20, 2021. https://www.abovetopsecret.com/forum/thread1302194/pg1.

Pagán, Camille Noe. "Cognitive Behavioral Therapy (CBT) for Negative Thinking & Depression." *WebMD* October 2020. https://www.webmd.com/depression/guide/cognitive-behavioral-therapy-for-depression.

"Panic Attacks and Panic Disorder." *Mayo Clinic.* Mayo Foundation for Medical Education and Research. 4 May 2018. https://www.mayoclinic.org/diseases-conditions/panic-attacks/symptoms-causes/syc-20376021 (2022).

"Panic Disorders." *Penn Medicine* https://www.pennmedicine.org/for-patients-and-visitors/patient-information/conditions-treated-a-to-z/panic-disorders. (2022)

Bibliography

Rabins, PV and Gallo JJ. "Depression without Sadness: Alternative Presentations of Depression in Late Life." *American Family Physician.* U.S. National Library of Medicine. https://pubmed.ncbi.nlm.nih.gov/10498109/.

Raypole, Crystal. "Where Toxic Shame Comes From and How to Work Through It." *Healthline.* https://www.healthline.com/health/mental-health/toxic-shame 23 September 2020.

Robinson, David. "Ecclesiastes 4:9—Teamwork Makes the Dreamwork." *Guide Magazine.* Blog. November 2017. https://www.guidemagazine.org/stories/5107-ecclesiastes-4-9-teamwork-makes-the-dreamwork

Rock, David and Heidi Grant. "Why Diverse Teams Are Smarter." *Harvard Business Review.* 19 March 2019. https://hbr.org/2016/11/why-diverse-teams-are-smarter.

"Science behind Trauma: Closing the Gap between what we know and what we do." *Multiplying Connections.* February 13, 2014. https://www.multiplyingconnections.org/science-behind-trauma.

Schilling, Mary Kaye. "A.J. Jacobs Loved His Morning Coffee so Much, He Thanked Everyone Who Made It. and We Mean Everyone!" *Newsweek.* 22 November 2018. https://www.newsweek.com/thanks-thousand-j-jacobs-coffee-radical-gratitude-1222245

Schimelpfening, Nancy. "Grief vs. Depression: Which Is It?" *Verywellmind.* Updated 23 January 2021 https://www.verywellmind.com/grief-and-depression-1067237

"Self-Esteem Mapped in the Human Brain." *University College London news. EurekAlert!* https://www.archive.eurekalert.org/pub_releases/2017–10/ucl-smi102017.php.

Sheldon, John. *Beyond Belief Sobriety.* https://beyondbeliefsobriety.com/videos/how-william-james-inspired-the-12-step-movement/. text below video para. 1.

Shulman, Lisa. "Healing Your Brain after Loss: How Grief Rewires the Brain." *American Brain Foundation.* 27 Aug. 2021, https://www.americanbrainfoundation.org/how-tragedy-affects-the-brain/

"Stress and Your Health." *MedlinePlus.* U.S. National Library of Medicine. https://medlineplus.gov/ency/article/003211.htm

Substance Abuse and Mental Health Services Administration. 2014. *Trauma-Informed Care in Behavioral Health Services.* Treatment Improvement Protocol (TIP). Series 57. HHS. No. (SMA) 13–4801. Rockville, MD. pp 33–52,61–75.

Svoboda, Martin (ed). "Quotes of Famous People." *Quotepark.* Blog. January 10, 2022. https://quotepark.com/quotes/2114049-robin-williams-people-dont-fake-depression-they-fake-being-okay/

Taylor, Janet *ABC News* "Oscar-winning actress Viola Davis says she struggles with 'imposter syndrome.'" https://abcnews.go.com/Entertainment/oscar-winning-actress-viola-davis-struggles-impostor-syndrome/story?id=45789758. February 28, 2017.

"Types of Grief and Loss." *CaringInfo.* 3 June 2021. https://www.caringinfo.org/planning/grief-and-loss/types-of-grief-and-loss/.

Bibliography

Van Dijk, Milenna T., et al. "Association of Multigenerational Family History of Depression with Lifetime Depressive and Other Psychiatric Disorders in Children." *JAMA Psychiatry*. vol.78, no.7, 2021, 778. https://doi.org/10.1001/jamapsychiatry.2021.

Volkow, Nora. *National Institute of Drug Abuse*. https://archives.drugabuse.gov/news-events/nida-notes/2003/03/dr-nora-d-volkow-named-nida-director.

Wax, Dustin. *Lifehack*. https://www.lifehack.org/articles/featured/11-ways-to-think-outside-the-box.html. July 21, 2021.

"What Does Ecclesiastes 4:9 Mean?" *Knowing Jesus* Verse of the Day. https://dailyverse.knowing-jesus.com/ecclesiastes-4-9.

"What Is Forgiveness?" *Hopeline*. Blog. https://www.thehopeline.com/forgiveness-is/.

Wise, M. "Oh What a Tangled Web We Weave When First We Practice to Deceive . . ." *European Psychiatry* 64, (2021) https://doi.org/10.1192/j.eurpsy.2021.89

Youn, Soo. "Robin Williams: 'Autopsy Confirms Death by Suicide." *The Hollywood Reporter*. November 7, 2014. https://www.hollywoodreporter.com/news/general-news/robin-williams-autopsy-confirms-death-746194/

www.ingramcontent.com/pod-product-compliance
Lightning Source LLC
Chambersburg PA
CBHW071838090426
42737CB00012B/2288